Ilita Fernandez

my **revision** notes

WJEC EDUQAS GCSE (9–1)

RELIGIOUS STUDIES

ROUTE B

Andrew Barron
with Joy White

HODDER EDUCATION
AN HACHETTE UK COMPANY

Imprimatur: + Vincent Nichols (Archbishop of Westminster)

Nihil obstat: Terry Tastad (Censor)

Date: 20 January 2018

The *Nihil Obstat* and *Imprimatur* are a declaration that a book or pamphlet is considered to be free from doctrinal or moral error. It is not implied that those who have granted the *Nihil Obstat* or *Imprimatur* agree with the contents, opinion or statements expressed.

The Publishers would like to thank the following for permission to reproduce copyright material.

Photo credits: Page 14 © Creedline/stock.adobe.com; **page 16** © Borisb17/stock.adobe.com; **page 35** © Bill Perry/stock.adobe.com; **page 53** © Granger Historical Picture Archive/Alamy Stock Photo.

Acknowledgements: The Bible: Quotations from THE HOLY BIBLE, NEW INTERNATIONAL VERSION®, NIV® Copyright © 1973, 1978, 1984, 2011 by Biblica, Inc.® Used by permission. All rights reserved worldwide.

Every effort has been made to trace all copyright holders, but if any have been inadvertently overlooked, the Publishers will be pleased to make the necessary arrangements at the first opportunity.

Although every effort has been made to ensure that website addresses are correct at time of going to press, Hodder Education cannot be held responsible for the content of any website mentioned in this book. It is sometimes possible to find a relocated web page by typing in the address of the home page for a website in the URL window of your browser.

Hachette UK's policy is to use papers that are natural, renewable and recyclable products and made from wood grown in sustainable forests. The logging and manufacturing processes are expected to conform to the environmental regulations of the country of origin.

Orders: please contact Hachette UK Distribution, Hely Hutchinson Centre, Milton Road, Didcot, Oxfordshire, OX11 7HH. Telephone: +44 (0)1235 827827. Email education@hachette.co.uk Lines are open from 9 a.m. to 5 p.m., Monday to Friday. You can also order through our website: www.hoddereducation.co.uk

ISBN 978 1 5104 1835 6

First published in 2018 by
Hodder Education,
An Hachette UK Company
Carmelite House
50 Victoria Embankment
London EC4Y 0DZ
www.hoddereducation.co.uk

Impression number 10 9 8

Year 2022 2021

Cover photo © tonyoquias/Alamy Stock Photo

Typeset in Bembo Std Regular 11/13pts. by Aptara, Inc.

Printed in Spain

A catalogue record for this title is available from the British Library.

Get the most from this book

Everyone has to decide his or her own revision strategy, but it is essential to review your work, learn it and test your understanding. These Revision Notes will help you to do that in a planned way, topic by topic. Use this book as the cornerstone of your revision and don't hesitate to write in it – personalise your notes and check your progress by ticking off each section as you revise.

Tick to track your progress

Use the revision planner on pages iv and v to plan your revision, topic by topic. Tick each box when you have:

- revised and understood a topic
- tested yourself
- practised the exam questions and gone online to check your answers.

You can also keep track of your revision by ticking off each topic heading in the book. You may find it helpful to add your own notes to the page at the back of the book as you work through each topic.

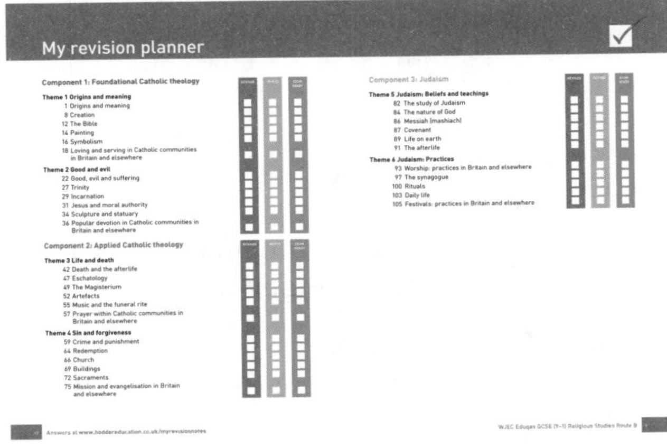

My revision planner

Component 1: Foundational Catholic theology

Theme 1 Origins and meaning

1 Origins and meaning
8 Creation
12 The Bible
14 Painting
16 Symbolism
18 Loving and serving in Catholic communities in Britain and elsewhere

Theme 2 Good and evil

22 Good, evil and suffering
27 Trinity
29 Incarnation
31 Jesus and moral authority
34 Sculpture and statuary
36 Popular devotion in Catholic communities in Britain and elsewhere

Component 2: Applied Catholic theology

Theme 3 Life and death

42 Death and the afterlife
47 Eschatology
49 The Magisterium
52 Artefacts
55 Music and the funeral rite
57 Prayer within Catholic communities in Britain and elsewhere

Theme 4 Sin and forgiveness

59 Crime and punishment
64 Redemption
66 Church
69 Buildings
72 Sacraments
75 Mission and evangelisation in Britain and elsewhere

Component 3: Judaism

Theme 5 Judaism: Beliefs and teachings

82 The study of Judaism
84 The nature of God
86 Messiah (mashiach)
87 Covenant
89 Life on earth
91 The afterlife

Theme 6 Judaism: Practices

93 Worship: practices in Britain and elsewhere
97 The synagogue
100 Rituals
103 Daily life
105 Festivals: practices in Britain and elsewhere

Answers at www.hoddereducation.co.uk/myrevisionnotes

WJEC Eduqas GCSE (9–1) Religious Studies Route B

Features to help you succeed

Key concepts

Clear, concise definitions of the key concepts from the specification are provided where they first appear.

Useful words

Clear, concise definitions of useful words are provided where they first appear.

Now test yourself

These short, knowledge-based questions provide the first step in testing your learning.

Sources of wisdom and authority

Quotations from key religious sources will support your understanding of religious beliefs.

Exam focus

Example answers to exam style questions with activities to help you improve your exam technique are provided for each component.

Exam practice

Practice exam questions are provided for each component. Use them to consolidate your revision and practise your exam skills.

Knowledge check

All of the key concepts for each topic are presented in a table to help you check that you know these essential definitions.

Summary questions

These short, knowledge-based questions will help you to consolidate your knowledge at the end of each topic.

Online

Go online to check your answers at www.hoddereducation.co.uk/myrevisionnotes

My revision planner

Component 1: Foundational Catholic theology

Component 2: Applied Catholic theology

Component 3: Judaism

A note on the authors

Andrew Barron is the Schools RE Advisor for the Diocese of Hexham and Newcastle. He wrote Components 1 and 2 as well as all the exam-style questions in this book.

Joy White is an experienced RE teacher, advisor, author and examiner. She wrote the Judaism content for Component 3 but has not written any exam-style questions in this book.

Assessment structure

EDUQAS GCSE Religious Studies requires students to complete three component examination papers:

Component 1: Foundational Catholic Theology
Written examination: 1 hour 30 minutes
37.5% of qualification

Candidates will study the following two themes:

Theme 1: Origins and Meaning

Theme 2: Good and Evil

This component will be assessed by compulsory questions focusing on knowledge, understanding and evaluation of the identified themes.

Component 2: Applied Catholic Theology
Written examination: 1 hour 30 minutes
37.5% of qualification

Candidates will study the following two themes:

Theme 1: Life and Death

Theme 2: Sin and Forgiveness

This component will be assessed by compulsory questions focusing on knowledge, understanding and evaluation of the identified themes.

Component 3: Study of Judaism
Written examination: 1 hour
25% of qualification

Candidates will study the beliefs, teachings and practices of Judaism.

This component will be assessed by compulsory questions focusing on knowledge, understanding and evaluation of the subject content.

Answering questions

There are four types of questions you will be asked.

Question	Command words	Marks	Point/level marked
a Define ...	In Component 1 and 2 – What do Catholics mean by ...? In component 3 – What do Jews mean by ...?	2	Point marked
b Describe ...	Describe a belief, teaching, practice, event etc.	5	Level marked
c Explain ...	Demonstrate knowledge and understanding of a topic by **explaining** the statements made with reasoning and/or evidence, e.g. Explain why ... Explain the main features of ... Explain the importance/significance of ... Explain teachings/beliefs/attitudes about ... Component 1 ONLY, asks for TWO Religious perspectives. Questions will be phrased: Explain from Catholic, Christianity and Judaism or two Christian traditions. Two religious responses are enough.	8	Level marked

Question	Command words	Marks	Point/level marked
d Discuss ...	'Statement.' Discuss this statement showing that you have considered more than one point of view. (You must refer to religion and belief in your answer.) Component 1 Origins and Meaning section must include non-religious beliefs. (You must refer to religious and non-religious beliefs such as those held by Humanists and Atheists, in your answer.) You may refer to non-religious views if it lends itself to the answer in other **d** questions.	15	Level marked

Each question will tell you the amount of marks it is worth.

This should help you to decide how much time to spend on it as well as the depth of your answer.

The space in the exam booklet will give you an idea of how much to write, although it isn't expected that you will fill it all.

Make sure you read the question carefully. It will give you some important cues about what to include in your answer to get the most marks.

Question a

These questions are worth 2 marks. Marks are allocated as follows:

1 mark for providing a limited definition

2 marks for giving and accurate and appropriate definitions.

Question b

Band	Band descriptor	Mark total
3	An excellent, coherent answer showing knowledge and understanding of the religious idea, belief, practice, teaching or concept. An excellent understanding of how belief influences individuals, communities and societies. Uses a range of religious/specialist language, terms and sources of wisdom and authority extensively, accurately and appropriately.	4–5
2	A good, generally accurate answer showing knowledge and understanding of the religious idea, belief, practice, teaching or concept. A good understanding of how belief influences individuals, communities and societies. Uses religious/specialist language and terms and/or sources of wisdom and authority generally accurately.	2–3
1	A limited statement of information about the religious idea, belief, practice, teaching or concept. A limited understanding of how belief influences individuals, communities and societies. Uses religious/specialist language and terms and/or sources of wisdom and authority in a limited way.	1
0	No relevant information provided.	0

Question c

Band	Band descriptor	Mark total
4	An excellent, highly detailed explanation showing knowledge and understanding of the diversity of the religious idea, belief, practice, teaching or concept. An excellent understanding of how belief influences individuals, communities and societies. Uses a range of religious/specialist language, terms and sources of wisdom and authority extensively, accurately and appropriately.	7–8
3	A very good, detailed explanation showing knowledge and understanding of the diversity of the religious idea, belief, practice, teaching or concept. A very good understanding of how belief influences individuals, communities and societies. Uses a range of religious/specialist language, terms and sources of wisdom and authority accurately and appropriately.	5–6
2	A good, generally accurate explanation showing some knowledge and understanding of the diversity of the religious idea, belief, practice, teaching or concept. A good understanding of how belief influences individuals, communities and societies. Uses religious/specialist language and terms and/or sources of wisdom and authority generally accurately.	3–4
1	A limited and/or poorly organised explanation showing limited knowledge and understanding of the diversity of the religious idea, belief, practice, teaching or concept. A limited understanding of how belief influences individuals, communities and societies. Uses religious/specialist language, terms and/or sources of wisdom and authority in a limited way.	1–2
0	No relevant information provided.	0

Component 1 Question 1d

Band	Band descriptor	Mark total
5	An excellent, highly detailed analysis and evaluation of the issue based on detailed knowledge of religion, religious teaching and moral reasoning to formulate judgements and present alternative or different viewpoints. An excellent understanding of how belief influences individuals, communities and societies. An excellent, highly detailed consideration of non-religious beliefs, such as those held by Humanists and Atheists. Uses and interprets religious/specialist language, terms and sources of wisdom and authority extensively, accurately and appropriately.	13–15
4	A very good, detailed analysis and evaluation of the issue based on accurate knowledge of religion, religious teaching and moral reasoning to formulate judgements and present alternative or different viewpoints. A very good understanding of how belief influences individuals, communities and societies. A very good, detailed consideration of non-religious beliefs, such as those held by Humanists and Atheists. Uses and interprets religious/specialist language, terms and sources of wisdom and authority appropriately and in detail.	10–12
3	A good, generally detailed analysis and evaluation of the issue based on a generally accurate knowledge of religion, religious teaching and moral reasoning to formulate reasonable judgements and recognise alternative or different viewpoints. A good understanding of how belief influences individuals, communities and societies. A good, reasonably detailed consideration of non-religious beliefs, such as those held by Humanists and Atheists. Uses and interprets some religious/specialist language, terms and/or sources of wisdom and authority.	7–9
2	Limited statement(s) of more than one viewpoint based on limited knowledge of religion, religious teaching and moral reasoning to formulate judgements. A limited understanding of how belief influences individuals, communities and societies. A limited consideration of non-religious beliefs, such as those held by Humanists and Atheists. Uses limited religious/specialist language, terms and/or few sources of wisdom and authority.	4–6
1	A poor, basic statement of a point of view and a very limited attempt or no attempt to formulate judgements or offer alternative or different viewpoints. Tenuous attempt or no attempt made to demonstrate how belief influences individuals, communities and societies. A very basic consideration or no consideration of non-religious beliefs, such as those held by Humanists and Atheists. Poor use or no use, of religious/specialist language, terms and/or sources of wisdom and authority.	1–3
0	No relevant point of view stated.	0

All other d questions

Band	Band descriptor	Mark total
5	An excellent, highly detailed analysis and evaluation of the issue based on detailed knowledge of religion, religious teaching and moral reasoning to formulate judgements and present alternative or different viewpoints. An excellent understanding of how belief influences individuals, communities and societies. Uses and interprets religious/specialist language, terms and sources of wisdom and authority extensively, accurately and appropriately.	13–15
4	A very good, detailed analysis and evaluation of the issue based on accurate knowledge of religion, religious teaching and moral reasoning to formulate judgements and present alternative or different viewpoints. A very good understanding of how belief influences individuals, communities and societies. Uses and interprets religious/specialist language, terms and sources of wisdom and authority appropriately and in detail.	10–12
3	A good, generally detailed analysis and evaluation of the issue based on a generally accurate knowledge of religion, religious teaching and moral reasoning to formulate reasonable judgements and recognise alternative or different viewpoints. A good understanding of how belief influences individuals, communities and societies. Uses and interprets some religious/specialist language, terms and/or sources of wisdom and authority.	7–9
2	Limited statement(s) of more than one viewpoint based on limited knowledge of religion, religious teaching and moral reasoning to formulate judgements. A limited understanding of how belief influences individuals, communities and societies. Uses limited religious/specialist language, terms and/or few sources of wisdom and authority.	4–6
1	A poor, basic statement of a point of view and a very limited attempt or no attempt to formulate judgements or offer alternative or different viewpoints. Tenuous attempt or no attempt made to demonstrate how belief influences individuals, communities and societies. Poor use or no use, of religious/specialist language, terms and/or sources of wisdom and authority.	1–3
0	No relevant point of view stated.	0

Origins and meaning

Key concepts

Creation *ex nihilo* means creation out of nothing. Before God created the universe, nothing existed. Only God can create out of nothing.

Omnipotence is the belief that God is all powerful.

Catholic beliefs about the origin of the universe and the concept of creation

REVISED

Catholic beliefs about creation

- Christians refer to the act of God bringing the universe into being as creation. Nothing existed before God created it.
- Only God creates, because he is **omnipotent** or all powerful.
- This idea of creating out of nothing is called in Latin, ***creation ex nihilo***.
- This belief can be found in the Bible. It can also be found in the writing of St Augustine.

Sources of wisdom and authority

You, O Lord [...] made something in the beginning, which is of yourself, in your wisdom, which is born of your own substance, and you created this thing out of nothing. You created heaven and earth but you did not make them of your own substance. If you had done so, they would have been equal to your only-begotten Son, and therefore to yourself, and justice could in no way admit that what was not of your own substance should be equal to you.

(St Augustine, *Confessions* xii, 7)

Now test yourself

TESTED

Read the extract from St Augustine.

1 What does it tell us about God and his role in creation? How does this agree with Genesis?

Differing Christian attitudes to the creation story

The story of creation was written thousands of years before modern science existed. Christians understand the story in different ways, depending on whether they interpret the Bible text literally or non-literally.

Some Christians take a fundamentalist approach. They believe that the account of creation as it appears in the Bible is an accurate account of what happened – this belief is known as creationism. They believe that the creation of the world and everything in it took place in six calendar days, exactly as the book of Genesis says. This stems from the view that the Bible is the inspired word of God, which is never mistaken.

Some Christians think that the creation story is not meant to be taken literally. Some try to harmonise the scientific and biblical accounts, claiming that each 'day' of the creation story is actually billions of years.

Catholics read the stories of creation in a symbolic way, believing that they reveal some important things about the nature of the world and humanity. Although the two accounts of creation in Genesis have different details, they share the same truths.

Jewish beliefs about creation

In Jewish belief, God is the creator and source of all life. Each week Jews celebrate the Sabbath, recalling that God made the world in six days and rested on the seventh.

Jews share the two stories of creation with Christians as these stories are in Genesis, which is also the first book of the Torah, the Jewish holy book. Some Orthodox Jews believe these stories are true accounts. They were revealed to Moses by God. Others, like Reform Jews, think that the creation accounts are stories which shouldn't be taken as historical facts.

Some Orthodox Jews have difficulty accepting modern scientific ideas. They reject evolution and the Big Bang theory. Others believe that God started the universe through the Big Bang and has guided the creation of life through evolution. They still have faith in God as a sustainer and provider.

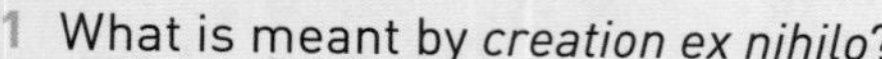

Now test yourself

TESTED

1 What is meant by *creation ex nihilo*?
2 What is a creationist?
3 Explain how creationists and Catholics differ in their ideas about the creation of the world.
4 Explain the similarities and differences between Jewish and Catholic explanations of creation.

The origin of the universe

REVISED

The Big Bang theory

- The branch of science which studies the origins of the universe is called cosmology.
- The current scientific thinking about the creation of the world is that it was caused by the big bang.
- This claims that all matter was originally concentrated into a tiny point which, as a result of a massive explosion in space 13.7 billion years ago, expanded into the universe and is still expanding today.
- This explosion, or big bang, caused particles and atoms to be formed. This led to the formation of stars and planets.
- This theory has led some people, such as Stephen Hawking, to doubt the existence of God completely, saying that we can explain the origins of the world without the need for a creator God.
- Powerful telescopes can detect evidence of background radiation which is thought to be left over from the initial expansion at the start of the universe.

The Catholic view of the Big Bang theory

- Catholics are happy to accept the Big Bang, as this theory supports their belief that God created the universe out of nothing.
- Many Christians accept the scientific explanations, but say that we must understand Genesis symbolically, not as a scientific explanation of the beginning of the world, but as a theological statement about the world's relationship to God.
- In fact, the Big Bang theory was put forward by a Catholic priest, Father Georges Lemaître.
- Science explains how the universe came about and Genesis explains why the universe began.

Is there a conflict between science and religion?

Many people think that science and religion are in conflict over the origins of the universe. This is not the case. There is only a problem if a person chooses to interpret the Bible literally. For creationists they are very critical of scientific ideas because they appear to contradict the truth that God has formed all life through his own power.

Even if the scientific view is correct in saying that the universe began with a big bang, have they really solved the question of 'where does the universe come from?' It is reasonable to ask what caused the big bang. Christians would argue that this is God.

Now test yourself

TESTED

1. What is the Big Bang?
2. Explain Catholic views on the Big Bang.
3. Explain why a creationist might have a problem with the Big Bang theory.

The theory of evolution and Catholic beliefs about creation

REVISED

Key concept

Evolution is the process of mutation and natural selection which leads to changes in species over time to suit particular environments.

Scientific theories of evolution

- According to science, life came about as a result of a process known as **evolution**.
- This idea was proposed by Charles Darwin.
- This is the idea that organisms gradually change and develop into new species by a process known as 'natural selection'.
- Certain characteristics help animals to survive. As they breed and pass these traits on over generations, it leads to new species developing.
- This is a process which takes millions of years to come about.
- The theory of evolution is supported by fossil record, which reveals that a large number of species have died out.
- DNA research shows that there are many similarities between species.

Richard Dawkins

- A modern supporter of this view is Richard Dawkins.
- Dawkins is an Atheist and believes evolution does away with the need for God and the belief that humans have souls.
- Dawkins argues that each living organism's body is just a survival machine for its genes and does not serve any other purpose.
- Humans are just a genetic mutation and are just advanced animals.

The Catholic view of evolution

- Some Christians do not accept the theory of evolution; they see it as an attack on their faith, especially if they read the Bible literally.
- Catholics do not interpret the Bible literally. Genesis needs to be understood symbolically.
- Pope John Paul II restated the view of pope Pius XII that there is no conflict between evolution and the teaching of the Christian faith.
- What is important to Catholics is not whether God chose to create through the process of evolution over many millions of years, but that in Genesis, God created with purpose (purposeful creation) and so everything that exists is part of his loving plan.
- This is what is important for Catholics to understand; not how it happened but why it happened.

The Pope's message sees no conflict between evolution and Catholic belief.

Sources of wisdom and authority

In his encyclical *Humani generis* (1950), my predecessor Pius XII has already affirmed that there is no conflict between evolution and the doctrine of the faith regarding man and his vocation [...] Taking into account the scientific research of the era, and also the proper requirements of theology, the encyclical *Humani generis* treated the doctrine of 'evolutionism' as a serious hypothesis, worthy of investigation and serious study.

(Pope John Paul II's message to the Pontifical Academy of Sciences: on evolution, 22 October 1996, paragraphs 3–4)

Now test yourself

TESTED

1. In a few sentences, explain what evolution means.
2. What scientific evidence supports the theory of evolution?
3. Describe Catholic attitudes to evolution.
4. Explain how Richard Dawkins' views challenge Catholic beliefs.

Catholic views on the origin and sanctity of human life

REVISED

Sanctity of life

- Most people, religious or not, would accept that human life is special and should be cared for.
- Catholics believe each person is unique because God made them.
- The creation of humans was unlike the rest of creation because they were made in a unique way and in the image of God. The Latin term for 'in the image of God' is ***imago Dei***.
- The Catholic Church teaches that all human life is sacred and that everyone has a right to life which should be protected and valued at every stage.

Key concept

Imago Dei means 'in the image of God'. It means that the belief that human beings are uniquely a reflection of God's personhood. Unlike the other animals, human beings are rational, free and moral.

Saint Catherine of Siena – the image of God (*imago Dei*)

The source here contains a conversation between a soul and God. The 'her' she refers to is the soul. The soul is made in the image of God.

St Catherine had a deep faith. She spent her life with outcasts and sinners showing them that they were created and loved by God. She has two important messages from her writing:

- **Humans come from God** – in the same way that children come from their parents or your reflection in the mirror shows you: 'Her dignity is that of her creation, seeing that she is in the image of God.'
- **Love** – God creates out of love. The fact that humans are made with dignity and in God's image shows how much he loves them. 'You are taken with love for her, for by love indeed you created her.'

Jewish beliefs about the sanctity of life

For Jews, God is creator, he alone gives and takes life. Genesis (the first book of the Torah) teaches that humans are created in the image of God (Genesis 1: 26–27) and life is precious. In the Tenakh there are references to a relationship with God even before birth (Psalm 139) and Jeremiah (1). The Ten Commandments, believed to have been given to Moses, also forbid the taking of a life.

Sources of wisdom and authority

Her dignity is that of her creation, seeing that she is the image of God, and this has been given her by grace, and not as her due. In that same mirror of the goodness of God, the soul knows her own indignity, which is the consequence of her own fault.

What made you establish man in so great a dignity? Certainly the incalculable love by which you have looked on your creature in yourself! You are taken with love for her; for by love indeed you created her, by love you have given her a being capable of tasting your eternal Good.

(St Catherine of Siena, specifically *The Dialogue of St Catherine of Siena*, 'A treatise of discretion')

Now test yourself

TESTED

1. What is the meaning of *imago Dei*?
2. Explain what St Catherine of Siena's writings say about the idea of *imago Dei*.
3. Explain whether Jewish beliefs about the sanctity of life are similar to Catholic beliefs.

The abortion debate

REVISED

Abortion is the deliberate ending of a pregnancy.

Different views on abortion

Abortion has been widely debated since it was legalised in Britain in 1967. Those against abortion think it is morally unacceptable to kill unborn babies. Others argue if a baby is going to be born with a severe illness or disability it would be kinder to permit an abortion.

A key question in the debate is, 'when does a person become a person?' Some argue from the moment of conception. Therefore, terminating a pregnancy is the same as murder.

Others would argue a person only 'begins' when they are first aware of their own existence or when independent life is possible. Therefore, terminating a foetus is not the same as murder.

The debate splits broadly into two camps:

Pro-life	Pro-choice
The idea that abortion is always wrong and every human (including embryos) has a right to life.	The idea that a woman should be able to choose what happens to her own body. This includes choosing to end a pregnancy.

The Catholic Church and abortion

- The Catholic Church is against abortion in all circumstances.
- Catholics believe human life is sacred.
- The Catholic Church teaches that life begins at conception.
- It is God who gives life at this moment and it is the start of a human being's relationship with God.
- Abortion is therefore seen as murder, a great moral evil, which is against one of the Ten Commandments: 'Do not murder.'
- The foetus has a right to life and termination is a great moral evil.
- Instead of having an abortion the Church would encourage those in this situation to give a child up for adoption.
- If a mother's life is in danger during the pregnancy (for example ectopic pregnancy) then action to save the life of the mother even if it threatens or destroys the life of the unborn child is acceptable. The intention is to save the mother, the effect on the child is not directly intended but is a side effect. This is known as the Principle of Double Effect.

Other Christian views on abortion

There is no single view on abortion in Christianity. Some fundamentalist Christians think abortion is never acceptable. Most Christians agree that it is not a good thing, but sometimes it is 'the lesser of two evils'. Some situations where some Christians might consider abortion as the 'lesser of two evils' include:

- If the pregnancy is the result of rape, an abortion might be the best option for the quality of life of the woman.
- If continuing the pregnancy might be dangerous to the woman's physical or mental health, then abortion should be allowed.
- If the child is likely to be severely disabled and so effect its quality of life.

Now test yourself

TESTED

1. Explain the Catholic approach to abortion.
2. Explain why some Christians think abortion is 'the lesser of two evils'.
3. Explain the difference between 'pro-life' and 'pro-choice'.

Humanist views on abortion

REVISED

There is not one single Humanist view on abortion. Humanists value happiness and personal choice. In making a decision they would look at the evidence, consequences and rights and wishes of everyone involved. Life is not sacred but is worthy of the highest respect. Generally, they would take a pro-choice stance and many Humanists campaigned for abortion to be legalised in in the 1960s so that unsafe, illegal abortions shouldn't take place. At the heart of the debate is whether the rights of the foetus outweigh the rights of the mother. Quality of life would be seen as more important than preserving life at all costs. Humanists believe that abortion is often the most morally acceptable choice to make.

Ultimately, it is a personal choice which should be made considering all the facts and consequences.

A Humanist's view about sanctity of life – Peter Singer

- Peter Singer is a Humanist and has some controversial ideas in relation to abortion and the value of life.
- He argues that even though all human life has value, it is not of equal value.
- If a person has no ability to think, relate to others or experience then their life has limited value.
- Therefore, embryos and newborn babies are all examples of biological but 'non-person' humans.
- Therefore, it is morally acceptable to take the lives of these 'non-person' humans if it will bring about less suffering and greater happiness.
- This not only applies to abortion, but also euthanasia (allowing someone suffering from a serious illness to die). A brain-dead person has no real value and therefore euthanasia is acceptable.

Speciesism

- Singer argues a conscious animal such as a dog, has more mental capacity and is more of a 'person' than a baby or an elderly person with dementia.
- Singer argues that animals have similar responses to humans, in that they feel pleasure and pain and therefore their interests must be taken into account.
- Therefore, arguing that human life is more important than any other type of life is wrong. This is the same as being racist. It is discriminatory and 'speciesist'.

Catholic response to Singer's views

Catholics would argue that humans remain a 'person' whether they are conscious or not, even when they are asleep, in a coma or haven't yet been born.

Catholics would agree that animals should be treated with care and looked after. As stewards of creation they have an obligation to do this. However, humans were made in the image and likeness of God, therefore they have a dignity which animals do not have.

Now test yourself

TESTED

1. Explain what Catholics believe about the sanctity of life.
2. Explain how a Humanist might disagree with the Catholic view on the sanctity of life.
3. What is meant by 'speciesism'?

Creation

Comparison of the first and second creation accounts

REVISED

- The first book of the Old Testament, Genesis 1–3, gives two accounts of creation.
- Most Catholics read the stories of creation in a symbolic way, believing that they reveal some important things about the nature of God and humanity.

The first account of creation: Genesis 1:1–2:3

A summary of Genesis 1:1–2:3	
Day 1	God created light and separated it from the darkness. God named the light 'day' and the darkness 'night'.
Day 2	God created the sky. God used the sky to divide the water that covered the earth into two halves.
Day 3	God created the sky. God used the sky to divide the water that covered the earth into two halves. God created dry land. The water he called 'seas' and the ground 'land'.
Day 4	God created the sun, moon and stars to light up the sky, govern night and day and mark the passing of time.
Day 5	God created all the species of animals that live on earth.
Day 6	God created the human beings and put them in charge of everything on the earth that had been created.
Day 7	God rested, blessed the seventh day and made it holy. The universe was complete.

What does this account tell us?

This account emphasises the greatness of God as creator of the universe:

- Transcendence – God exists above and beyond creation which makes him unlike anything else that exists.
- Eternal – that God creates heaven and earth 'In the beginning', shows that he already existed, God has no beginning.
- **Omnipotent** – God is all powerful, creation happens just by him commanding it (Gen 1:3). Before he creates nothing exists. He creates from nothing, creation *ex nihilo*.

Key concept

Omnipotence means the belief that God is all-powerful.

The second account of creation: Genesis 2:4–24

A summary of Genesis 2:4–24
God created a man, called Adam, out of dust and breathes life into him.
God provides him everything he needed in the Garden of Eden, but told him not to eat the fruit of the tree of the knowledge of good and evil.
God creates all the creatures and Adam names them all but none are suitable to be his partner.
God puts Adam to sleep and creates Eve, a woman, from his rib.
Their lives were perfect until they disobeyed him, which led to God banishing them from the Garden of Eden forever.

What does this account tell us?

As well as agreeing with many of the themes of the first account this one shows God is:

- **Omnibenevolent** – God creates out of love. He needs nothing but provides everything humans need. God does not want man to be lonely so he creates other species to keep him company, and he allows Adam to name them, but he knew that these were not suitable companions for Adam so he created Eve and they became one flesh.
- **Immanent** – This means that God is not distant from the world, but is involved in it, he is close to the first humans and does everything for them.

Now test yourself

TESTED

1 Explain the differences between the accounts of creation in Genesis 1 and Genesis 2.
2 Explain what the accounts of creation tell us about God and humans.

Catholic beliefs about nature of human beings and their relationship with creation

REVISED

In both narratives the message is that human life is special and sacred. Humans are different from all other animals and have a special responsibility to take care of the world.

- **Sanctity of life** – humans are created last in Genesis 1 and are the high point of God's creation. In Genesis 2 God personally creates Adam and Eve, Adam from the dust of the earth and Eve from Adam's rib. As part of his creation, God reflects again that all that he has made is good which includes human beings.
- **Image of God** – humans were created *imago Dei* – in the image of God, 'So God created mankind in his own image, in the image of God he created them.' (Gen 1:27) which makes them sacred and holy and unlike any other animal.
- **Stewards of God's creation** – God commands that humans have authority over nature and a responsibility to take care of it. In Genesis 1 God creates humans to rule over his creatures. In the second Genesis account Adam is put in the garden to 'work it and take care of it' but his authority is seen when God asks him to name all the animals.

Key concept

Stewardship is the duty to care for creation responsibly, as stewards rather than consumers, and to protect it for future generations.

Sources of wisdom and authority

Then the Lord God formed a man from the dust of the ground and breathed into his nostrils the breath of life, and the man became a living being.

So the Lord God caused the man to fall into a deep sleep; and while he was sleeping, he took one of the man's ribs and then closed up the place with flesh. Then the Lord God made a woman from the rib he had taken out of the man, and he brought her to the man. The man said, 'This is now bone of my bones and flesh of my flesh; she shall be called 'woman,' for she was taken out of man.' That is why a man leaves his father and mother and is united to his wife, and they become one flesh.

(Genesis 2:7, 21–24)

Sources of wisdom and authority

'Let us make mankind in our image, in our likeness, so that they may rule over the fish in the sea and the birds in the sky, over the livestock and all the wild animals, and over all the creatures that move along the ground.'

So God created mankind in his own image, in the image of God he created them; male and female he created them.

God blessed them and said to them, 'Be fruitful and increase in number; fill the earth and subdue it. Rule over the fish in the sea and the birds in the sky and over every living creature that moves on the ground.'

(Genesis 1:26–28)

Now test yourself

TESTED

Copy and complete the table below with a definition of each term and how it is shown in the creation accounts in the Bible.

Concept	Meaning	How it's shown in the creation accounts
Stewardship		
Imago Dei		
Sanctity of life		

The importance of preserving the planet and caring for the environment for Catholics

REVISED

In both stories of creation, human beings are the most important part of creation, but they are still creatures and therefore part of Creation. They are not the Creator, but God made humans superior to the rest of Creation by giving them reason and free will. This is the reason why God made humans stewards of the world.

Therefore Catholics should be concerned about looking after the environment and the planet. Catholics need to work to protect the planet, cutting down on pollution, care for animals and make sure that the world is in the best shape to pass on to future generations.

For Christians the two greatest commandments are to love God and to love their neighbour. The idea of neighbour means not just those close to us, but people in different countries. Catholics should be concerned about those who suffer badly from climate change.

The Catholic Church also teaches that every individual has a duty to contribute to the good of society. This is called the common good. Catholics should act justly and seek justice for others, especially the poor. This approach is most likely to lead to good things for everyone, as everyone would benefit from living in a healthy, well cared-for environment.

Humanist attitudes to creation and stewardship

REVISED

Humanists would agree with Christians that we need to look after the world, but for different reasons. For Humanists, human life has come about randomly because of evolution. No creator God is needed. Humans can use their reason to make ethical decisions. This is what makes humans superior to other animals. Human beings can act to give their lives meaning by seeking happiness in this life and helping others to do the same. They would say we need to be stewards of the world out of a concern for human beings and other animals, not because we were commanded to do it by a creator God. They would say we should work for a more sustainable world, causing as little harm to the environment as possible. This position is based on reason not because God has commanded it.

Now test yourself

TESTED

1. Explain why Christians believe they should care for the environment.
2. Give two examples of practical things a Christian could do to help the environment.
3. What are the similarities and differences between Catholic and Humanist beliefs in the environment?

The Bible

Catholic understanding of the nature of revelation and inspiration

REVISED

Catholics believe that the Bible is the inspired word of God. God made use of specific people who wrote in a human language, and did so at a particular time and place in history. Not everything they wrote might have been historically or literally accurate. Catholics must work carefully to determine exactly what a sacred author is saying to be true, and when an author is writing metaphorically using as an image to help bring out the truth more clearly.

This is seen as the Holy Spirit giving **inspiration** to believers, who respond by accepting the message and sharing it with other people. For believers, the Bible has a great authority as the message comes from God, impacting how they live they lives. All Christians should be guided by the teachings in the Bible.

> **Key concepts**
>
> **Inspiration** refers to 'God breathed'. The belief that the Spirit of God guides an individual to act or write what is good and true.
>
> **Revelation** is the word used to describe all of the ways in which God makes himself known to human beings. Christians believe that God does this finally and fully in the person of Jesus Christ.

The structure of the Bible

The Christian Bible is divided into two main parts: the Old Testament and the New Testament. The word testament means an agreement or a promise. So, the Old Testament deals with how God looked after the Jewish people and the New Testament deals with how God sent his Son, Jesus, for the whole world. The Old Testament was written mainly in Hebrew, the Jewish language, and the New Testament in Ancient Greek.

The Old Testament

The Old Testament is made up of the following types of writing (literary forms):

- **The laws (Torah)** – the first five books of the Bible (Pentateuch) deal with how the Jewish people became God's chosen race and how God taught them to live. These books tell of the creation and the lives of the patriarchs, such as Abraham. They also teach about Moses and the laws given to the people of Israel, including the Ten Commandments.
- **History** – there are twelve historical books in the Bible, such as Joshua and Judges. These books show how God guided his people even though they were not always ready to listen.
- **Wisdom** – Psalms is the prayer book of the Jewish people. There are also books of religious and moral teaching, such as the Book of Proverbs, which contains sayings about many aspects of life.
- **Prophets** – from time to time God sent inspired figures to challenge the Jews to remain faithful to God.

The New Testament

The New Testament is based on the life and teachings of Jesus and the apostles to whom Jesus taught God's message. All the New Testament was written in Greek.

It can be divided into four types of writing (literary forms):

- **The Gospels** (Matthew, Mark, Luke and John) – these are the most important books of the Bible for all Christians, as they tell Jesus' story. The word 'gospel' means 'good news' – the good news about Jesus.
- **The Acts of the Apostles** – this is the sequel to Luke's Gospel. It tells the story of the Early Church, after Jesus' resurrection.
- **The letters** (or Epistles) – these were written mainly by Paul, but also by Peter, James, John and Jude. They were Christian leaders writing to Christians giving them advice on how to put Jesus' teaching into practice and explaining what it means to be a Christian.
- **The Book of Revelation** – this is the last book in the Bible, dealing with John's vision of heaven and the defeat of evil.

Origins of the Bible

It took about 350 years for the books that we now know as the Bible to be accepted as authentic records of Christian beliefs. The Synod of Hippo in 393CE decided which texts should be included in the Bible. For a book to be accepted into the New Testament it had to fit the following rules:

- It had to be accepted by all Christians.
- The work had to go back to the apostles.
- It had to have an early date.
- It had to agree with other presentations of Christian beliefs.

The words of the Bible have been very carefully preserved over the centuries. The first Bibles were hand written and copies were made so other people could read them.

Now test yourself

TESTED

1. List and describe each of the literary forms you find in the Old and New Testaments.
2. Explain why the Bible is a source of authority for Christians.
3. Explain how the Bible came into being.

Different Christian views on Genesis

Some Christians believe that the Bible is the literal word of God. For example, they believe that God created the world in a single week and that everything was made perfectly at that time. They reject the theory of evolution. They believe the Holy Spirit dictated the Bible and that no one should question anything that the Bible teaches because it comes from God. Where there appear to be contradictions, they think that this just shows that people do not yet have enough understanding. This approach rejects any kind of compromise with science.

For Catholics, Genesis 1–3 has to be considered as a myth. It is not meant to be read as literally true. It is a story that, while not being 'true', contains great 'truths'. As a result, there is no problem accepting evolution and the Big Bang as the Bible is not a science book. The creation story in Genesis is a poetic reflection on the significance of God as creator.

Now test yourself

TESTED

1. Explain how a Catholic might interpret the story of Creation from Genesis 1–3.
2. Explain how Orthodox and Reform Jews differ in their understanding about the Book of Genesis.

Jewish beliefs: the Torah

The Torah is the first five books of the Tenakh (Torah, Nevi'im and Ketuvim) and is believed to be the holiest and most important part of scripture for Jews. Moses is believed to have received the Torah from God on Mount Sinai.

For Orthodox Jews they believe it was given by God to Moses and must be taken literally and not changed. Many Orthodox Jews will seek to obey the *mitzvot* as duties in life. Society may change but Jewish teachings don't. The Torah was given in its entirety to Moses and can never be changed.

For many Reform and Liberal Jews, it is not necessary to take the scriptures literally and they believe that sometimes they have to be adapted for modern life.

Painting

Christianity has a long tradition of sacred art using themes and images from Christian belief. The use of art goes back to the time when people could not read or write. Learning about Jesus or the Bible was made easier by looking at pictures, images or statues. The artist would use their artwork to express their views. To add to this the person looking at it could study it and reflect upon it over time.

- Catholic art is used to express faith in God and to glorify him.
- Art can be used as a focus for prayer and meditation.
- Artwork demands a personal response, so it helps people to think and reflect on their own beliefs.
- Art can sometimes challenge people; an artist's interpretation of a Biblical theme or belief might make the viewer rethink or reinforce their beliefs.

Michelangelo's *Creation of Adam*

REVISED

The Sistine Chapel in the Vatican, Rome, where the cardinals vote for a new pope, was painted by Michelangelo between 1508 and 1512. Michelangelo was a very religious man. Not only are the paintings very beautiful giving glory to God, they are intended to start reflection and meditation about Catholic beliefs about God.

There are nine scenes from Genesis on the ceiling. The most famous is the *Creation of Adam*. God is shown as an old bearded man enveloped in a swirling cloak. Adam is naked and positioned on the lower left. God's right arm is extended as if giving the spark of life into Adam, whose left arm is extended in a mirroring pose of God's. The mirroring pose shows humanity's creation in God's image. The fingers of Adam and God do not touch indicating that God, the giver of life, is reaching out to Adam with life.

Adam	Meaning
• Adam is on the left of the painting, lying back on the earth from which he has been formed as described in Genesis: 'then the lord God formed man of dust from the ground, and breathed into his nostrils the breath of life; and man became a living being.' (Genesis 2:7) • Adam is a perfect human being; young, handsome and strong. • Adam resembles God, like a son looks like his father. • Adam mirrors the pose of God.	• Humans were created by God. • God created a perfect world. • Humans are made in the image and likeness of God.
God	**Meaning**
• God is presented as a dynamic, active figure as if he is hard at work at his greatest creation. God reaches out to the more passive figure of Adam. • God is shown as older than Adam, yet he is strong and powerful.	• The viewer is reminded of the belief that God is both eternal and all powerful. • The difference in age between Adam and God also signifies the parent-child relationship that exists between God and humanity, God is the Father of all creation.
Hand	**Meaning**
• Adam and God are seen reaching out to touch each other with their fingertips.	• The touch of fingertips represents the spark of life given to all humans by God; human life is sacred and a gift from God.
Cloud	**Meaning**
• God is on a cloud, carried by a group of angels. This is a contrast to Adam on earth. • Some believe the cloud is in the shape of a brain showing God is the source of all knowledge and wisdom. • Others believe that the cloud represents a womb because of the red background. Also, the green cloth hanging down could be the umbilical cord.	• This shows the greatness and transcendence of God. • God is omniscient. • This signifies the idea that God gives all life, in the same way that the womb gives life to a new child.

How the *Creation of Adam* expresses Catholic beliefs about creation, God and humans

Michelangelo's *Creation of Adam* reflects many of the principal Catholic beliefs about creation.

- God is all powerful and **transcendent**.
- God made each human being in his own image (*imago Dei*).
- Humans are God's greatest creation.
- Life is a gift from God.
- God is a loving father who cares about his creation.

Key concept

Transcendence means existing outside of space and time; God exists in a way that makes him nothing like anything else that exists, above and beyond creation.

Now test yourself

TESTED

1. List the key parts of Michelangelo's *Creation of Adam*.
2. For each of the parts of the *Creation of Adam* you have listed in question 1, write one or two sentences explaining their meaning.
3. Explain how the *Creation of Adam* expresses the idea of *imago Dei*.
4. Explain how the *Creation of Adam* expresses the idea that God is transcendent.

Symbolism

The *Tree of Life Apse* mosaic at San Clemente

REVISED

The tree of life mosaic can be found in the apse of the Church of San Clemente in Rome. An apse is a semi-circular dome which is positioned above the altar in a church. It dates to the twelfth century.

The mosaic is filled with symbolism. The central image is a cross which merges with many other important symbols.

The cross and the tree

The cross is a crucifixion scene with Mary and St John beside it and the hand of God the Father above, offering a wreath of victory to Christ.

The apostles are represented in several different ways in the mosaic. First, the apostles appear as doves surrounding Jesus on the cross. In the Catholic faith doves are symbols of peace and a sign of the Holy Spirit filling the earth on Pentecost.

At the base of the cross is a tree, considered to be the tree of life. The tree of life is a reference from Revelation 22:2. '[...] on either side of the river, the tree of life with its twelve kinds of fruit, yielding its fruit each month; and the leaves of the tree were for the healing of the nations.'

Through the crucifixion, people of all nations are saved. In this way, religious viewers will recognise the cross as a symbol of the death of Christ to absolve humanity of their sins.

Some may also see the cross as being the tree of life: this can be seen with the way the cross emerges out of the tree and is then wrapped with the vines. Branching out from the tree on both sides are swirling vines that cover the entire mosaic branching out to all of humanity.

The tree is also a reminder of the tree of knowledge of good and evil in the Garden of Eden. Adam and Eve ate the fruit bringing sin and death into the world. Jesus reverses the disobedience of Adam by being obedient to God and offering his life on the cross. St Paul writes about this, calling Jesus the New Adam. Adam went against God and brought pain, suffering and sin into the world. Jesus was faithful to God and brought a way back to God and a new way to be human.

> Thus it is written, 'The first man, Adam, became a living being'; the last Adam became a life-giving spirit. But it is not the spiritual that is first, but the physical, and then the spiritual. The first man was from the earth, a man of dust; the second man is from heaven.
> (1 Corinthians 15:45–47)

Alpha and omega and Chi-Rho

Above the cross is the Chi-Rho symbol with the Greek letter alpha and omega either side of it.

- Chi-Rho – the symbol looks like the letters X and P, which are the first two letters of the word Christ in Greek. It is a very early symbol of Christianity and can be viewed as the first Christian cross.
- The alpha and omega – they are the first and last letters of the Greek alphabet. This reminds Christians that God is the beginning and ending of all things. In the Book of Revelation, God speaks of himself as the alpha and omega and from early Christian times it was also used to refer to Jesus. We are therefore being reminded that Jesus is eternal because he is God.

The lamb

At the bottom of the cross there are twelve lambs who are facing towards a lamb at the centre of the picture directly under the cross. This central lamb is the 'lamb of god' or Jesus.

A lamb is a symbol of sacrifice. In the story of the Passover in the Old Testament, a lamb was sacrificed and its blood put on the doorposts of the homes of the Israelites. The Angel of Death 'passed over' these houses and instead killed the first-born sons of the Egyptians. The event is celebrated by Jews every year in the feast known as the Passover. The Israelites had been saved from slavery.

Jesus is described as the 'lamb of God' because his death on the cross saved humanity from their sin and death, just like the sacrificed lamb had saved the Israelites.

The twelve lambs are the apostles. They also lived a sacrificial life, they gave up their homes and families to follow Jesus and spread the word after his death.

The four evangelists

Above the apse are symbols for the four evangelists (Matthew, Mark, Luke and John).

- The image for Matthew is a man. Matthew is the Gospel of Christ's humanity and his humbleness and humility are highlighted throughout the book.
- The image for Mark is a winged lion. The winged lion, which signifies leadership and royalty, is therefore seen as a symbol for Christ as king.
- The image for Luke is a winged ox. An ox was used in sacrifice in the Temple. The winged ox is a reminder of the priestly character of Jesus and of his sacrificial death for the sins of all mankind.
- The image for John is a flying eagle. An eagle is of the sky. This book is totally unlike the three other gospels in that it begins with a high theological meditation upon the meaning of the fact of Christ.

Now test yourself

TESTED

1 Copy and complete the table to the right, explaining the meaning of the symbols found in the tree of life apse mosaic.
2 For each of the four evangelists (Matthew, Mark, Luke and John) explain:
   a What they are depicted as in the mosaic.
   b Why they are depicted as this.
3 Explain why is Jesus sometimes called the 'new Adam'.

Symbol	Meaning
The tree	
The dove	
The alpha and omega	
The Chi-Rho	
The lamb	

Loving and serving in Catholic communities in Britain and elsewhere

Catholic social teaching

REVISED

Catholic social teaching is a set of principles about building a just and fair society.

Teachings about human dignity

At the heart of Catholic social teaching is human dignity. Catholics believe that humans were created in the image and likeness of God, and that each human life is sacred. This is linked to Jesus' teaching that we must 'love our neighbour, as we love ourselves.' Catholics take a strong position on issues connected with the beginning and ending of life (abortion and euthanasia), but this belief has a huge impact on how Catholics support people with disabilities, how they address global inequality and their approach to civil rights issues.

Teachings about justice, peace and reconciliation

Peace and reconciliation are at the heart of the gospel. Catholic social teaching condemns the arms trade and supports those who refuse to take up arms on grounds of conscience. It looks towards the kingdom of God and tries to find ways we can create a lasting peace in the world, a peace that is experienced and learnt about from a relationship with God.

The common good

The Church promotes the idea of the common good. This means seeking the conditions in society that promote the fulfilment of all people, both as individuals and as groups. In order for people to flourish and reach their potential, society needs to promote respect for human rights and the dignity of each person, space to develop spiritual and material well-being, and peace and security within society.

Sources of wisdom and authority

Since all men possess a rational soul and are created in God's likeness, since they have the same nature and origin, have been redeemed by Christ and enjoy the same divine calling and destiny, the basic equality of all must receive increasingly greater recognition [...] with respect to the fundamental rights of the person, every type of discrimination, whether social or cultural, whether based on sex, race, colour, social condition, language or religion, is to be overcome and eradicated as contrary to God's intent. For in truth it must still be regretted that fundamental personal rights are still not being universally honoured [...] Therefore, although rightful differences exist between men, the equal dignity of persons demands that a more humane and just condition of life be brought about [...] Human institutions, both private and public, must labour to minister to the dignity and purpose of man. At the same time let them put up a stubborn fight against any kind of slavery, whether social or political, and safeguard the basic rights of man under every political system.

(*Imago Dei* in *Gaudium et spes* 29 and 78)

Now test yourself

TESTED

1. Explain why Catholics believe in human dignity.
2. Explain why Catholics believe they should work for peace, justice and reconciliation.
3. What is meant by the common good?
4. Summarise the key messages of *Gaudium et spes* 29 and 78 in your own words.

Interfaith dialogue

REVISED

Britain: a multi-faith society

- The UK has a strong Christian heritage, but modern Britain is a multi-faith society, including Muslims, Jews, Hindus, Sikhs and Buddhists.
- In the UK people have religious freedom which means it is up to the individual to choose which religion they practise or not.
- Atheism, not believing in God, is much more common now.

What is interfaith dialogue?

This means co-operative, constructive and positive engagement between people of different faiths and people of no faith such as Humanists and Atheists, to:

- promote mutual understanding, respect, tolerance and harmony
- identify common ground
- engage in shared action for the common good of society.

Why do we need interfaith dialogue?

Living in a multi-faith society brings many benefits. Different religious cultures and traditions bring with them a variety of food, clothes, music and literature into our lives. With this comes new ways of living and enjoying life. By living and working alongside those from other religious backgrounds we can gain greater tolerance, respect and understanding towards those who have a different viewpoint to us. This leads to harmony and a safe and happy society.

The Catholic Church and interfaith dialogue

- Catholics believe they have a duty to put across the Gospel message.
- They believe non-Christian religions have some truth, but only Christianity has the whole truth.
- Other religions should be respected.
- All people are created in the image of God (*imago Dei*).
- The popes have spoken out about the importance of respect and tolerance between different faiths. For example, Pope Benedict said, 'Together with all people of good will, we aspire to peace. That is why I insist once again: interreligious and intercultural research and dialogue are not an option but a vital need for our time.' (February 2007)
- The Vatican II Council stressed the importance of dialogue with Jews and Muslims.

Now test yourself

TESTED

1 What is the meaning of interfaith dialogue?
2 Explain why interfaith dialogue is important for Catholics.

Catholic charities

REVISED

Being a Catholic isn't limited to prayer, or things they might do on Sundays. It is about putting faith into action, and involves every aspect of life. Catholic charities try to reflect Catholic beliefs that:

- humans were created in the image and likeness of God, and that each human life is sacred
- this is linked to Jesus' teaching that we must 'love our neighbour, as we love ourselves'
- respect for human life means respecting all of God's creation.

Catholic Fund for Overseas Development (CAFOD)

The major Catholic agency working for world development and supported by the Catholics of England and Wales is CAFOD (Catholic Fund for Overseas Development). It was started by the Catholic bishops of England and Wales in 1962.

- CAFOD is an organisation which tries to live out the Church's mission on a global scale. It tries to help those in need. It promotes long-term development so that less-developed countries can support themselves.
- CAFOD also has a disaster fund to help natural disasters and refugees. Emergency aid might mean sending food, medicines and shelters to victims of a disaster, or sending blankets and food to war refugees.
- About five per cent of CAFOD's budget is spent on educating the people and churches of England and Wales about the need for development and the ways in which Catholics can help less-developed countries.
- CAFOD works for social justice challenging unfairness and tries to bring an end to poverty.

St Vincent de Paul Society (SVP)

The St Vincent de Paul Society is an organisation of Catholics who try to help those in need in the UK. Small groups of the SVP, known as conferences, are found in many parishes, schools, universities and hospitals across the UK. Their activities may be any or all the following:

- Regular visiting and personal care to help families who are finding it difficult to organise their family or home.
- Helping the lonely or bereaved and the housebound.
- Visits to individuals and families, to the sick at home or in hospitals and hospices, to residential homes and to offenders' institutions.
- Visiting housebound elderly people to prevent them from feeling isolated. Many appreciate a friendly face and enjoy a chat over a cup of tea.
- Shopping, decorating, gardening, filling in official forms and making sure people are receiving their statutory benefits.
- Organising children's camps for children from poor or troubled homes, and holiday schemes to provide a break for family carers, to give poor families a holiday or a break.
- Organising stores for unwanted furniture, which can be used when housing the homeless.
- Providing drop-in centres to give lonely people an opportunity to socialise.

Young Vincentians are the younger members of the St Vincent de Paul Society. The SVP has a successful programme in primary schools called 'Mini Vinnies'. For secondary school-aged youth they have Youth SVP.

Now test yourself

1. Explain, with an example, how the work of CAFOD reflects Catholic beliefs about the dignity of human beings.
2. Explain, with an example, how the work of SVP reflects Catholic beliefs about loving your neighbour.

TESTED

Knowledge check

Question a) is always about definitions of key concepts. Make sure you know them.

Use the look, cover, write and check technique to learn them. Look at the concept. Cover it and then write it down. Finally check your answer.

Creation ex nihilo	Creation out of nothing. Before God created the universe, nothing existed. Only God can create out of nothing.
Evolution	The process of mutation and natural selection which leads to changes in species over time to suit particular environments.
Imago Dei	In the image of God. The belief that human beings are uniquely a reflection of God's personhood. Unlike the other animals, human beings are rational, free and moral.
Inspiration	'God-breathed' The belief that the Spirit of God guides an individual to act or write what is good and true.
Omnipotence	The belief that God is all powerful.
Revelation	The word used to describe all of the ways in which God makes himself known to human beings. Christians believe that God does this finally and fully in the person of Jesus Christ.
Stewardship	The duty to care for creation responsibly, as stewards rather than consumers, and to protect it for future generations.
Transcendence	Existing outside of space and time. God exists in a way that makes him nothing like anything else that exists: above and beyond creation.

Summary questions

1 What does creation *ex nihilo* mean?
2 What is omnipotence?
3 How might a fundamentalist interpret the story of creation?
4 What do Christians believe about the Big Bang?
5 What do Jews believe about creation?
6 According to Genesis 1–2 how did God create the world?
7 How is this different to Genesis 3?
8 What is revelation?
9 What is inspiration?
10 What would you find in the Old Testament?
11 What would you find in the New Testament?
12 Where would you find stories about Jesus in the Bible?
13 What does *imago Dei* mean?
14 Explain what Chi-Rho is.
15 What is alpha and omega?
16 What is human dignity?
17 What is Catholic Social Teaching?
18 What is CAFOD? Give examples of what it does.
19 What is the SVP? Give examples of what it does.

Good, evil and suffering

Catholic perspectives on the origin of evil

REVISED

Key concepts

Evil is the absence of good and the impulse to seek our own desires at the expense of the good of others, which often results in suffering.

Free will is the decision-making part of a person's mind. A will is free if the person is able to choose right from wrong without being controlled by other forces.

Suffering is pain which harms human beings. Some suffering is caused by other human beings (often called 'moral evil'); some is not (often called 'natural evil').

The problem of evil for Catholics

Catholics believe in one God, who is/has:

- omnipotent (all-powerful)
- all-loving
- complete knowledge of past, present and future
- created a good world.

But if this is true, why does the world contain so much **evil** and **suffering**?

Catholic response to evil	
Free will	**Original sin**
• **Free will** is a gift from God. • Catholics believe that God created humans with the ability to choose between good and evil. • When humans choose the wrong thing it causes suffering. • Humans are to blame not God. They have abused their gift. Bad choices cause suffering. • Humans are not programmed robots. • What about suffering not caused by humans (i.e. natural as opposed to moral evil)?	• The story of Genesis tells how the world was created. • Adam and Eve decided to eat the forbidden fruit going against God's wishes. • This is the first (original) sin, sometimes known as the Fall. • As a result of this pain and suffering and natural suffering were introduced into a perfect world. • Since that time all humans have original sin, the tendency to go against God. • Original sin is a reminder that we all share some responsibility for the evil and suffering in the world.

St Augustine and evil

Sources of wisdom and authority

And in the universe, even that which is called evil, when it is regulated and put in its own place, only enhances our admiration of the good; for we enjoy and value the good more when we compare it with the evil.

For what is that which we call evil but the absence of good? Disease and wounds mean nothing but the absence of health; for when a cure is affected, that does not mean that the evils go away from the body and dwell elsewhere: they altogether cease to exist.

For the Almighty God, who has supreme power over all things, being himself supremely good, would never permit the existence of anything evil, if he were not so omnipotent and good that he can bring good even out of evil.

(St Augustine, *Enchiridion* 3,11)

In the Enchiridion, St Augustine gives three answers to the question of suffering:

Augustine's three answers to the question of suffering

1. St Augustine says that the existence of evil helps people to appreciate the good in the world. For example, being unwell helps us to appreciate when we are healthy.

2. St Augustine says that evil is just the absence of good things. This is called **privation**. God does not cause or permit evil because evil isn't even a thing.

3. St Augustine says God allows suffering because he is omnipotent and good. He allows evil because in his **goodness** and power he is always able to bring a greater good out of suffering. Suffering can be beneficial.

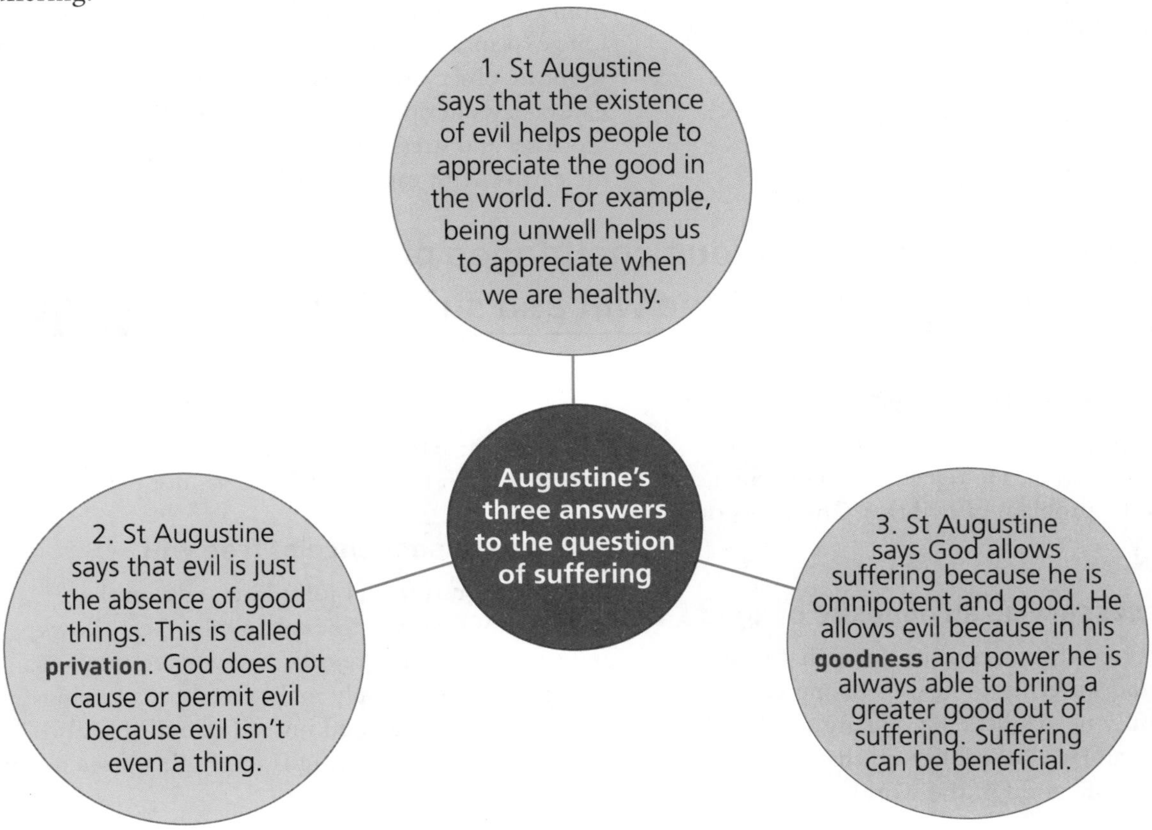

Key concepts

Goodness is the quality of being like God: seeking the well-being of others selflessly.

Privation is the loss or absence of a quality or something that is normally present. Evil is a privation of good.

Now test yourself

1 Explain why evil and suffering might be a problem for Catholics.

TESTED

Alternative views on the nature and origin of evil

REVISED

Non-Christian views on the nature of evil

For some the problem of evil is so big they reject God altogether. David Hume put forward the inconsistent triad. A 'triad' is a group of three things. The following group is 'inconsistent' because it seems that not all of them can be true at the same time:

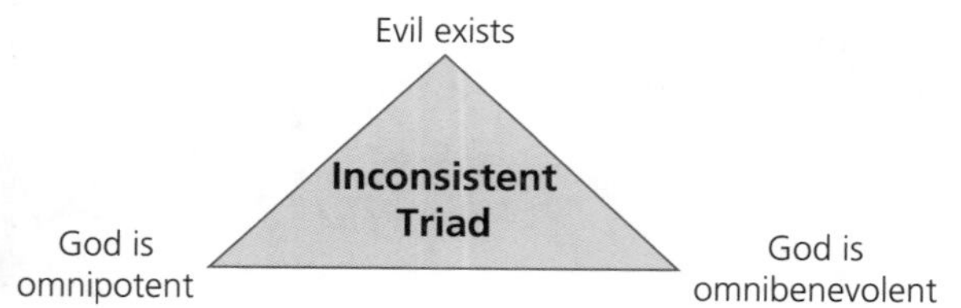

Hume concluded that either God does not exist or he is not worthy of worship.

Evil is divided into two categories:

Types of evil	
Moral evil	**Natural evil**
This is suffering which is a result of human action. Examples are theft, burglary, terrorism, assault, rape and murder.	This is suffering which is not to do with human actions, but with the way the world is. Examples are floods, volcanoes, cancer, disease and earthquakes.

Traditionally it is easier to explain moral evil as it is a result of human bad choices. It removes the blame from God. Natural evil is more difficult to explain. One explanation offered is the general laws argument: scientific observation means that there must be natural laws in operation. These laws describe innate processes and stresses such as, for example, stresses on the earth's crust causing earthquakes.

Philosophical and non-religious challenges posed by belief in God's goodness, free will and suffering

REVISED

Mackie, free will and evil

Atheist philosopher John Mackie (1917–81) took Hume's ideas further. He rejected some of the usual answers to the problem of evil that Christians often give.

Evil is necessary as an opposite of good

Mackie rejected this: even if it is true that we need some evil and suffering to help us to appreciate the good, we only need a little bit. He argues that there is far more and far worse suffering than is needed to contrast with the good in the world.

Evil helps us to become better people

Mackie also rejects the traditional Christian argument that suffering helps us to become better people. Why should God need to make us better through suffering? Why not just make us perfect to start with? Also, if this is true, then why does suffering often make people worse, not better?

Evil is a consequence of free will

Both St Augustine and John Hick rely on the existence of free will to explain why God allows evil to exist. Mackie rejects this: why couldn't an omnipotent God simply make free human beings who always choose good instead of evil? He also feels that evil and suffering is too high a price to pay for having free will.

Now test yourself

TESTED

1. What is the inconsistent triad?
2. What is the difference between moral and natural evil? Do they need different solutions?

Other Christian views on the nature and origin of evil

REVISED

St Irenaeus and John Hick

John Hick developed the ideas of St Irenaeus. According to Hick and Irenaeus, humans were made in the image of God, but are not perfect. They need to grow to become spiritually perfect. Suffering and evil is the best way for humans to develop. Through free choices they can learn to make the correct choices. The process of soul making is a response to evil in the world. This explains why God allows natural evil. This type of evil allows humans to grow and become better people.

Jewish beliefs about the nature and origin of evil

Jews do not believe that people are born evil (they do not share the Christian concept of original sin). For Jews evil and suffering are seen as a consequence of human beings' wrong choices.

Jews believe they are born free with the inclination to do good or to do evil, but that God has given human beings choices and they must struggle against the inclination to do evil actions and to obey God.

Catholic beliefs about the relationship between God's goodness and the goodness of the created world

REVISED

Catholics say that God is good and creation is good. But what does this mean? A complete understanding of God is beyond us, but analogy (moving from observation of the world around us to think about its creator) can help us to understand something of God. For example, although everybody is a sinner, we still see many signs of goodness in people: generosity, kindness, forgiveness and compassion. If this is human goodness then God the creator, in whose image humans are made, must be supremely good. Similarly we look at the world around us: at the oceans, the forests, the sky, and we marvel at its beauty. This teaches us something of the beauty of God, as 'the beauty of creation reflects the infinite beauty of the Creator' (Catechism of the Catholic Church 341).

Jewish beliefs about the goodness of God

Jewish views are very similar to those of Catholics. For Jews, God is the source of all life and referred to throughout the Torah as the only creator. The goodness of God is shown by the creation of the world and the giving of the Torah. Jews believe that God is the only God and is omnipotent. There is no belief in an opposite God. God cares about the world.

Now test yourself

TESTED

1 Copy and complete the table below, explaining the different responses of these key thinkers to the purpose of suffering.

Key thinker	Response to the problem of evil
St Augustine	
Hick and Irenaeus	
Hume	
Mackie	

The meaning of suffering and Catholic ambivalence

REVISED

Catholics generally hold that while suffering is always hard, it is not always evil. As a result, Catholics have an ambivalent attitude to suffering (that is, they have mixed feelings).

Christ's death and Isaiah 53

Catholic views on suffering stem from the Bible:

- In the Book of Job, God tells the suffering Job that he is just not capable of understanding the reasons why God chooses to do, or not do, certain things. Catholics must therefore trust that God understands the reasons for suffering.
- Isaiah 53 describes how the acceptance of suffering by a 'suffering servant' brought about salvation.

Moreover, when Christians suffer it is a way to bring them closer to an understanding of Jesus (and how his suffering and death ultimately brought about salvation) and a way to bring about a greater good. So, although suffering is horrible it can bring about good things. Ultimately, Catholics believe that suffering is a mystery and God uses suffering to bring about good. Even so, evil never becomes a good.

These factors shape how Catholics respond to suffering. Catholics share their suffering with God in prayer. During Mass Catholics pray for the sick, dying and those who are suffering, they ask God to help those in need. Catholics also help those who are suffering by giving to charity. Some Christians feel it is their vocation to be doctors or nurses and fight against suffering.

Jewish beliefs about suffering

For Jews, suffering comes from two different sources – humanmade and natural. Often suffering has arisen because God has given free will to people to do good or to do evil. Jews see evil and suffering as a consequence of human beings' wrong choices. Jews do not believe in original sin.

For Jews, God is the source of all life and referred to throughout the Torah as the sole creator. He is the judge and he is merciful. He will protect and care for all that he has created. The goodness of God is shown by the creation of the world and the giving of the Torah.

Jews have several solutions to the problem of suffering and evil. The biblical book of Job suggests that it is fruitless for humans to try and figure out why God causes people to suffer. Other traditional solutions include the idea that suffering isn't really bad. Jews interpret the 'suffering servant' in prophet Isaiah, as being about the Jewish people in general, which suggests that they suffer in order to redeem the wicked of humanity.

The Jewish people suffered very badly under Nazi Germany when millions of them were put to death in the Holocaust. There has been much reflection on this from 'God is hiding' to 'God is dead.'

Now test yourself

TESTED

1 Explain, with an example, how a Catholic might respond to the problem of evil and suffering.
2 Explain, with an example, how a Jew might respond to the problem of evil and suffering.

The Trinity

Christians believe the following things about God:

- There is only one God.
- God exists as three Persons: Father, Son and Holy Spirit.
- Each of these three Persons is distinct from the other two.
- Each of these three Persons is fully God.
- But there are not three Gods.

Catholics believe in one single God, who made himself known to the world as three distinct Persons: God the Father, God the Son (Jesus) and God the Holy Spirit. This is known as the doctrine of the Trinity, and is a fundamental belief for all Catholics. The way the Trinity works is considered to be a mystery, but it does help in understanding some of the qualities of God.

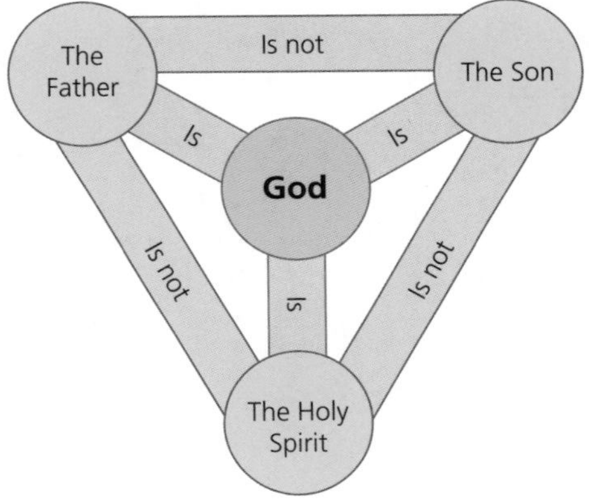

The Nicene Creed

The doctrine of the Trinity is set out in the Nicene Creed. Catholics believe that the Trinity works as one. Yet within this common purpose, each of the three Persons has a special role:

- God the Father created heaven and earth.
- God the Son, Jesus, is the saviour of the world.
- God the Holy Spirit is an invisible spiritual power who guides, helps and inspires human beings.

The importance of the Trinity for Catholics

The concept of the Trinity is very important to Catholics. Without a doctrine of the Trinity, it would not be possible for Christians to believe that Jesus is God. The belief that Jesus is God is probably the most important Christian belief.

The importance of the Trinity is demonstrated by its central role within religious practice. For example:

- The simplest of Catholic prayers, the sign of the cross, is trinitarian: 'In the name of the Father and of the Son and of the Holy Spirit.'
- Many prayers are said to or in the name of the Trinity. For instance, the Eucharistic prayer finishes with the words:

> Through him, and with him, and in him, O God almighty Father, in the unity of the Holy Spirit, all glory and honour is yours, for ever and ever. Amen.

The Nicene Creed is also recited by Catholics during prayer and worship, and at baptisms.

- This is a way of reminding worshippers of the main points of Christianity.
- The worshippers are declaring publicly that this is what they truly believe.
- The creed is said together by everyone – a sign that they share these beliefs.
- It binds them together as a group who share common beliefs.

Jewish beliefs

Jews agree with Catholics that there is one God. The belief in only one God is stated in the most important prayer for Jews: the Shema. It is also stated in the Ten Commandments. However, they do not accept Jesus as the Son of God or the idea of the Trinity. There are different attributes of God such as 'judge' and creator' but these are only characteristics of the one God. These attributes of God are not separate persons, but are just the different ways in which human beings experience God.

Historical development of the Trinity

REVISED

The word 'trinity' does not appear explicitly in the Bible. The doctrine of the Trinity developed over several hundred years. When the first Christians began to reflect on their experience of Jesus, they began to see that they experienced the one God in three different ways. They saw this in the scriptures.

Biblical support for the doctrine of the Trinity

The theological concept of the One God consisting of three divine Persons (Father, Son and Holy Spirit) is found many times in the New Testament, for example:

- 'Go therefore and make disciples of all nations, baptising them in the name of the Father and of the Son and of the Holy Spirit.' (Matthew 28:19)
- 'All things have been handed over to me by my Father; and no one knows the Son except the Father, and no one knows the Father except the Son and any one to whom the Son chooses to reveal him.' (Matthew 11:27)
- Jesus Christ as the divine word/logos, the light and life of the world, the 'only-begotten Son' of the Father. (John 1:1–18)
- We also see the Trinity at Jesus' baptism. (Mark 1:9–11)

Augustine's metaphorical explanation of the Trinity: as love, lover and beloved

St Augustine used a metaphorical explanation to explain the concept of the Trinity. Specifically, he used the idea that 'God is Love' (1 John 4:8) to explain the Trinity:

- Love needs three things: the person who is doing the loving, the person who is being loved and the love itself.
- These three aspects are present in God – even before God had made any creatures to love. So St Augustine says that the Trinity of Father, Son and Holy Spirit is like this Trinity of love, lover and beloved.

This idea of God as love is a helpful one for Christians because it makes it clear that love needs to be an important part of every Christian's life.

Sources of wisdom and authority

There are three things in love, as it were a trace of the Trinity ... love is of someone that loves, and with love something is loved. Behold, then, there are three things: he that loves, and that which is loved, and love.

(Augustine, *De Trinitate*)

Now test yourself

TESTED

1 Explain what is meant by the Trinity:
   a according to the Nicene Creed
   b according to St Augustine.
2 Explain why belief in the Trinity is important to Catholics.
3 How might Jews and Catholics disagree about the nature of God?

Incarnation

Meaning and significance of the Incarnation

REVISED

In Jesus, God the Son became a human being. It is called 'the **Incarnation**' because God became visible 'in the flesh' in the person of Jesus of Nazareth. The most usual way Christians express this belief is by calling Jesus the 'Son of God'. This connects to the doctrine of the Trinity, where the term 'Son' is used to name the second person of the Trinity. When Christians call Jesus the 'Son of God' they mean that he is God who has become a human being; that he is the 'incarnate Son'. Christians also believe that Jesus is 'fully God and fully human'. Christians believe that Jesus is one person, with two natures: one human nature, and one divine (which means 'godly') nature.

In the opening chapter of John's Gospel, John calls Jesus 'the Word' (the Word is God's creative power). The idea of the Incarnation is made very clear with the words, 'The Word became flesh and made his dwelling among us.'

In the ***kenosis*** hymn in Philippians, St Paul also shows how Jesus 'emptied himself' of his divine nature to become human.

Key concept

Incarnation means 'made flesh'. The Christian belief that God became man in the person of Jesus, fully human and fully divine.

Kenosis is a Greek word which means 'emptying'. It refers to the idea that Jesus gave up some of his divine attributes when he became human.

Scriptural origins of the Incarnation

REVISED

Sources of wisdom and authority

In the beginning was the Word, and the Word was with God, and the Word was God. He was in the beginning with God; all things were made through him, and without him was not anything made that was made.

(John 1:1–3)

And the Word became flesh and dwelt among us, full of grace and truth; we have beheld his glory, glory as of the only Son from the Father.

(John 1:14)

Sources of wisdom and authority

This passage is known as the *kenosis* hymn. *Kenosis* is a Greek word meaning to empty or pour out.

[...] who, though he was in the form of God, did not count equality with God a thing to be grasped, but emptied himself, taking the form of a servant, being born in the likeness of men. And being found in human form he humbled himself and became obedient unto death, even death on a cross.

(Philippians 2:5–8)

Jewish views

Jewish people do not accept that Jesus was God as this challenges their basic belief that God is one. This belief is stated in the Shema, which is a very important prayer for Jewish people. It is also stated in the Ten Commandments.

Now test yourself

1. What is meant by the Incarnation?
2. Explain what the following passages from the bible reveal about the Incarnation:
   a. John (1:1–3, 14)
   b. The *kenosis* hymn (Philippians 2:5–8)
3. What are the main similarities between the two passages?

TESTED

Incarnation and the problem of evil

REVISED

The mystery of why a good God allows pain and suffering is very hard to understand. A belief in the Incarnation is very important to Christians in helping them to respond to the problem of evil. Jesus' Incarnation and suffering give Christians a way of being able to continue to believe in the goodness of God, even in the face of human suffering.

The Incarnation is important to Christians because it means that God, as Jesus, can identify with human beings. Christians believe that the Incarnation is a demonstration of God's immense love for human beings. In Jesus, they see a God who loves them so much that he was willing to take on human form and sacrifice his human life for them. Jesus understands fully what it means to be human. Jesus is a comfort to those who suffer because Christians believe that Jesus is God's presence with his people. Christians believe Jesus is with us in our suffering because Jesus himself experienced suffering and did not run from it but bore it out of love. Christians may not understand why God allows the suffering to happen, but they should trust God because he knows what they are going through.

Christians should also follow Jesus' example. Jesus spent his life working against suffering. The best example of this is the way he cured the sick. Catholics should do what they can to help those who are suffering.

John Paul II, *Salvifici doloris*

Salvifici doloris is a document that was written by Pope St John Paul II. The title is Latin, meaning 'the saving power of suffering'. He says that the problem of evil is not easy to understand. The only way for humans to get an idea about it is to try and understand the depth of God's love for humans which Jesus showed through his willingness to die on the cross. He writes that if Christians willingly 'offer up' their own suffering in prayer for the sake of others, that they can share in the saving suffering of Jesus. If a Christian can do this, it is an act of love resembling Jesus' own act of sacrifice. This is very difficult to understand but Pope St John Paul II believes that if we try and bear our suffering patiently and offer it to God in prayer, that God will somehow be able to use it to bring about good for others.

Sources of wisdom and authority

But in order to understand the 'why' of suffering, we must look to the revelation of divine love [...] This answer has been given by God to human beings in the Cross of Jesus Christ.

Those who share in Christ's suffering have before their eyes the Paschal Mystery of the Cross and Resurrection, in which Christ takes on human weakness [...] But if in this weakness there is accomplished his lifting up, then the weaknesses of human suffering can be filled with the same power of God made visible in Christ's Cross.

(*Salvifici doloris*, 13 and 23)

Now test yourself

TESTED

1 Explain why the Incarnation is important to Catholics.
2 Describe what the *Salvifici doloris* says about suffering.
3 Explain how the Incarnation helps Catholics to deal with suffering.

Jesus and moral authority

Jesus' examples and teachings as the authoritative source for moral teaching

REVISED

Jesus' examples of moral behaviour

Catholics try to model themselves on Jesus. There are many examples of how Jesus acted and what he taught to inspire Christians today.

- Jesus gave us the Golden Rule – 'do to others as you would want them to do to you.' This is a summary of the Sermon on the Mount. 'So whatever you wish that men would do to you, do so to them; for this is the law and the prophets.' (Matthew 7:12)
- Jesus told his disciples to love. 'A new commandment I give to you, that you love one another; even as I have loved you, that you also love one another. By this all men will know that you are my disciples, if you have love for one another.' (John 13:34–35)
- Jesus showed this in the way that he healed the sick (Jesus cleanses a leper, Matthew 8:1–4) He also made the outcast and sinner welcome. (Jesus and Zacchaeus, Luke 19: 1–10)
- Jesus showed forgiveness to those who crucified him. (Luke 23:33–35)
- Jesus explains how his followers should behave in the Sermon on the Mount (Matthew 5–7).

Teachings of Jesus: the Beatitudes

Jesus also gives clear teachings on how people should live their lives. The clearest collection of these teachings is in chapters five to seven of Matthew's Gospel in a section that is often called the Sermon on the Mount.

- The sermon begins with a list of blessings, which are often called the Beatitudes (which is Latin for 'blessings').
- The key messages of the Beatitudes is that those who are closest to God are often those that the world does not recognise or value.

Sources of wisdom and authority

Blessed are the poor in spirit, for theirs is the kingdom of heaven.
Blessed are those who mourn, for they will be comforted.
Blessed are the meek, for they will inherit the earth.

(The Beatitudes, Matthew 5: 3–5)

How do the Beatitudes turn the values of the world on their head?

The fulfilment of the law: the Sermon on the Mount

Jesus is a source of moral authority as he came to fulfil God's law. Jesus says the requirements of being a follower of Jesus goes further and deeper than the Law of Moses (hence why the sermon is sometimes known as the 'fulfilment of the law'). Jesus repeats a phrase which begins: 'You have heard that it was said ...' and ends with 'But I say to you ...' Here Jesus shows the ways in which being a follower of his is more demanding than the religious Law (Torah) which his listeners have been living by. For example, murder was wrong, but now anger is unacceptable, adultery was wrong but now looking at someone lustfully is wrong. It isn't just about an action, intention and the reason behind it goes deeper.

Summary of the Sermon on the Mount

'Think not that I have come to abolish the law and the prophets; I have come not to abolish them but to fulfil them.' (Matthew 5:17)

Following Jesus requires a higher standard.

The old teaching	The new teaching
You have heard it said ...	**But I tell you ...**
Do not murder.	Don't be angry. Settle arguments quickly.
Do not commit adultery.	Do not look lustfully at a woman. If your eye causes you to sin, pluck it out.
Divorce is allowable.	No divorce except for sexual immorality.
Do not break oaths.	Do not make an oath. Let your 'yes' be 'yes' and your 'no, 'no'.
An eye for an eye, a tooth for a tooth.	Turn the other cheek.
Love your neighbour, hate your enemies.	Love your enemies, pray for those who persecute you.
Giving to the needy	Give in secret. Do not let the left hand know what the right hand is doing.
Prayer, fasting	Don't pray and fast for show – you've had your reward.

All of the above shows that it isn't enough to do the right thing. Your intention is everything.

Now test yourself

TESTED

1 List three examples of Jesus' moral teachings.
2 What is the meaning of the Beatitudes?
3 Explain how Catholics might use Jesus' teachings to help them make an ethical decision.

Other sources of moral authority

REVISED

Key concepts

Conscience is human reason making moral decisions. The knowledge we have of what is right and wrong and the God-given compulsion within all human beings to do what is right and to avoid what is evil.

Natural law is the moral laws of right and wrong which are universal and not dependent on human laws. The belief in natural law is the belief that the moral law is discoverable by every human being and is the same for all human beings in all places at all times.

Natural law

A belief in **natural law** is a key part of Catholic moral teaching. This is the idea that there is a discoverable moral law which applies to all humans. Natural law was put forward by St Thomas Aquinas. It says that all human beings have some purposes in common: preserving life, procreation, seeking the truth, living in society and worshipping God. Because of these common purposes, there are some universal laws that all human beings have to obey (for example, laws against murder, child abuse, theft and lying). At a basic level, humans should avoid evil and do good.

Catholics would say the ability to find out natural law shows the universe is created by a God who is good. The ability to recognise suffering as an evil is a sign that we have this God-given ability to tell the difference between good and evil.

Conscience

St Thomas Aquinas defined **conscience** as 'the mind of human beings making moral decisions.' The ability to discover natural law is what Catholics call 'conscience'. Catholics have an obligation to follow their conscience. Catholics must make sure their conscience is informed by the Bible and tradition as interpreted by the Church. Catholics making moral decisions must follow their conscience.

Catholics believe that if humans followed their conscience more often there would be far less moral evil in the world, and far less suffering as a result. The existence of conscience is another proof of the goodness of God who created human beings in his own image, and is sometimes given as a response to the problem of evil.

Virtues and suffering

Catholics believe that living a good life and obeying one's conscience is something that requires practice. Catholics believe that there are moral habits which human beings need to practice in order to become good people. These moral habits are called 'virtues' which comes from the Latin word for perfection. These virtues challenge our instinctive selfishness; our desire to keep ourselves safe has to be overcome in order to become more courageous, for example. People can grow in virtue through the experience of suffering. For example, 'If I suffer poverty, this can make me more generous when I do have food and other things to share.'

Now test yourself

1 Explain the meaning of natural law.
2 Explain how natural law and conscience are related.

TESTED

Sculpture and statuary

Sculpture and statues in Catholic tradition and worship

REVISED

A common feature in Catholic churches are statues. There will be a crucifix, a statue of Mary and a statue of the saint after whom the church is named. The crucifix is the most common focus for Catholic prayer and it reminds Catholics of the Incarnation, but also of the suffering of Jesus which, for Catholics, is a reminder of God's love for them. These statues will have places to kneel in front of them and places to light candles. The candles are called votive candles. They are symbols of the prayers the worshipper is offering.

Catholics do not pray to the statues. The statues are reminders of God and Jesus and these help them to focus their prayer on what really matters. Catholics would say that they do not pray to Mary and the saints but they ask Mary and the saints to intercede on their behalf and pray to God for them.

Other traditions

For many Christians, especially those who belong to some Protestant traditions, the making of religious statues goes against the second commandment that forbids the making of any image as an object of worship (Exodus 20:4–5). They might use a simple cross without a figure representing Jesus on it.

Jewish attitudes to statues

Jews do not use statues as a focus for prayer. It goes against the Ten Commandments: 'You shall have no other gods before me.' Synagogues do not have any representation of God as he is above human understanding.

Statues and suffering: Michelangelo's *Pietà*

REVISED

Statues help Catholics to reflect on the meaning of suffering. One of the most famous statues that does this is Michelangelo's *Pietà*. It is a statue of Mary holding the body of her son after his crucifixion. The word 'pieta' comes from the Latin word for holiness.

The two figures are beautiful and idealised, despite their suffering. This reflects the belief of Catholic ambivalence to suffering; that suffering is somehow a mirror of love and can be a source of blessing.

- Mary is depicted as youthful and peaceful instead of as a broken-hearted and older woman (as is often portrayed in earlier versions of the Virgin Mary).
- Mary seems at peace with what has happened to her son.
- Mary's left hand is positioned with an open palm, which is a sign that she accepts what has happened.
- Mary's figure is larger than that of Jesus. She comfortably cradles Jesus' body. This shows her as a mother because it is as if she is holding a baby in her arms.
- In supporting Christ, Mary's right hand does not come into direct contact with his flesh, it is covered with a cloth. This shows the sacredness of Christ's body.
- Christ is presented almost as if he is in a peaceful sleep, and not as if he has been bloodied and bruised after hours of torture.
- The wounds of Jesus are hardly visible.

Now test yourself

TESTED ☐

1. Explain why the crucifix is important to Catholics.
2. How might a Catholic person and a Jewish person disagree over the use of statues?
3. Explain what the *Pietà* reveals about a Catholic understanding of suffering.

Popular devotion in Catholic communities in Britain and elsewhere

The meaning and significance of pilgrimages for Catholics

REVISED

A pilgrimage is a journey to a holy place. Many Catholics still go on pilgrimages. The Catholic Church recognises sites of pilgrimage as among the most appropriate places for prayer.

There are many reasons for going on pilgrimage. These may include:

Life as a journey: pilgrimage as a response to human suffering

Going on a pilgrimage can help believers to reflect on their life's journey. It is an opportunity to take time out and focus on their journey to God. Often it is a journey of self-discovery, most noticeably for those who are sick. Very few sick people come back cured. However, they may come back feeling at peace and able to accept and cope with the problems they face. In this way, many people learn how to value the role of God in their lives in a new way.

Shrines to Mary

Many places of pilgrimage are dedicated to Mary, who Catholics call Our Lady. The most popular of these shrines in Europe are Lourdes (in France) and Fatima (in Portugal). Most shrines are in places where people have claimed to see visions of Mary. Catholics often pray to Mary at sites of pilgrimage, believing that she can pray to God on their behalf. The most well-known shrine to Mary in England is in Walsingham.

Lourdes

- One of the most popular shrines is Lourdes, in south-west France.
- In 1858, a young girl called Bernadette Soubirous had visions of Mary.
- Mary told Bernadette to dig for a spring.
- This spring is believed to have healing qualities and many pilgrims bathe there.
- Now thousands of pilgrims go to pray at the grotto.
- Large numbers of young people volunteer as helpers for the sick and disabled pilgrims, which can be a life-changing experience.
- It's a practical way that ordinary people can respond to the mystery of suffering.

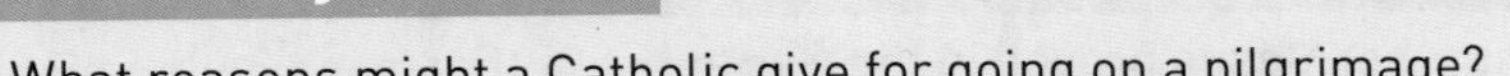

Now test yourself TESTED

1 What reasons might a Catholic give for going on a pilgrimage?
2 Explain why many places of pilgrimage are connected with Mary.

Popular piety

REVISED

Popular piety is a form of devotion. It refers to forms of worship or prayer that are inspired by culture rather than the liturgical worship of the Church. A good example is the rosary.

The rosary

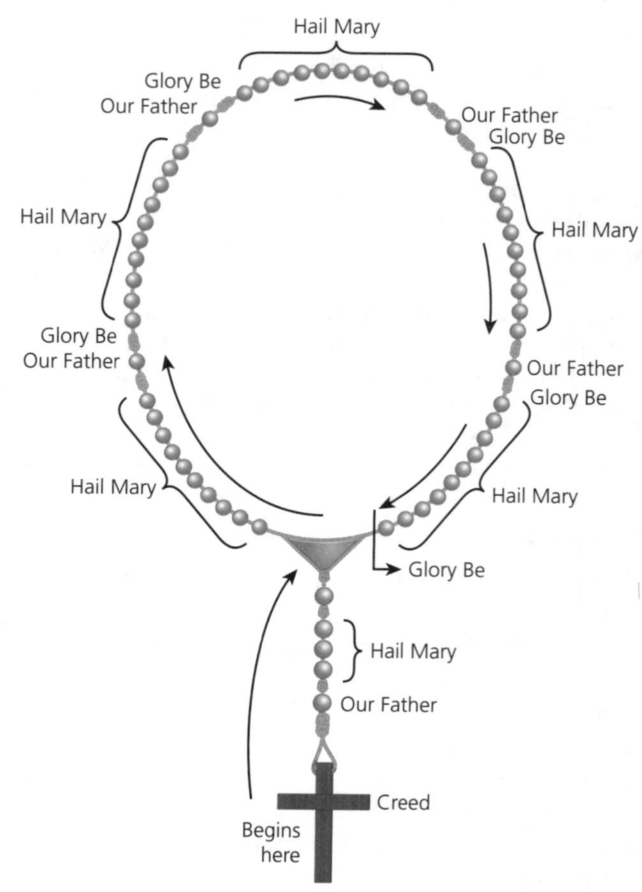

The rosary is a series of beads used by Catholics to help them concentrate during prayers. The rosary can be said as an individual or in a group. Each bead represents a prayer and the beads are arranged in a sequence of one 'Our Father', ten 'Hail Marys' and one 'Glory Be'. Most Catholics can recite these prayers from memory. The fact that they do not need to concentrate on what words to say means that they can think more deeply. Each sequence of beads is called a decade, and a set of rosary beads usually has five decades.

As they progress through the decades, Catholics reflect on some of the important events in the life of Jesus and of Mary. It is a form of meditation. These events, called mysteries, are in groups of five. For example, the joyful mysteries are the Annunciation, Mary's visit to Elizabeth, the birth of Jesus, the presentation of the baby Jesus in the temple and the finding of Jesus in the temple.

The sorrowful mysteries

There are five sorrowful mysteries, each of which focus on events associated with the suffering and death of Jesus.

Catholics can reflect on the suffering of Jesus. It helps them to find answers to the problem of evil	
The agony in the Garden	This is when Jesus prayed in the Garden of Gethsemane on the night before he died. He prayed to be spared the suffering he knew was to come but in the end accepted God's will out of obedience and love.
The scourging at the pillar	This is when Pilate had Jesus whipped in an attempt to satisfy those who wanted Jesus to be crucified. It didn't do any good and Pilate condemned Jesus to death.
The crowning with thorns	This is when the soldiers mocked Jesus, twisting thorns into a crown because he had been charged with claiming to be the King of the Jews.
Jesus is made to carry his cross	This is when Jesus carried his own cross to Golgotha, the place of his crucifixion.
Jesus is crucified and dies on the cross	This is when Jesus is nailed to the cross and, after six hours, dies on the cross.

Now test yourself

TESTED

1 Explain what a rosary is used for.
2 Explain how the sorrowful mysteries might help Catholics to respond to the problem of evil.

Knowledge check

Question a) is always about definitions of key concepts. Make sure you know them.

Use the look, cover, write and check technique to learn them. Look at the concept. Cover it and then write it down. Finally check your answer.

Conscience	Human reason making moral decisions. The knowledge we have of what is right and wrong and the God-given compulsion within all human beings to do what is right and to avoid what is evil.
Evil	The absence of good and the impulse to seek our own desires at the expense of the good of others which often results in suffering.
Free will	The decision-making part of a person's mind is called the will. A will is free if a person is able to choose right from wrong without being controlled by other forces.
Goodness	The quality of being like God: seeking the well-being of others selflessly.
Incarnation	'Made flesh' The Christian belief that God became man in the person of Jesus, fully human and fully divine.
Natural law	The moral laws of right and wrong which are universal and not dependent on human laws. The belief in natural law is the belief that the moral law is discoverable by every human being and is the same for all human beings in all places at all times.
Privation	The loss or absence of a quality or something that is normally present. Evil is a privation of good.
Suffering	Pain or loss which harms human beings. Some suffering is caused by other human beings (often called moral evil); some is not (often called natural evil).

Summary questions

1 What is the problem of evil?
2 What does privation mean?
3 Why is evil a problem for those who believe in God?
4 What is original sin?
5 What is free will?
6 Explain the difference between moral and natural evil.
7 Who are the three Persons of the Trinity?
8 Why do Jewish people not agree with the Trinity?
9 What is *kenosis*?
10 Explain the word Incarnation.
11 Why is the Incarnation important to Catholics?
12 How does the Incarnation help Catholics to deal with suffering?
13 What is the golden rule?
14 Would Jewish people agree with statues?
15 Why is a crucifix important to Catholics?
16 Why do people go on pilgrimages?
17 What happens at Lourdes?
18 What is conscience?

Exam focus

(a) questions

These questions are always about definitions of key concepts. You should know these very well.

They are worth two marks:

- One mark for a simple definition.
- Two marks for a definition with an example or a point which is developed.

a What do Catholics mean by revelation? (2)

The word used to describe all of the ways in which God makes himself known to human beings. Christians believe that God does this finally and fully in the person of Jesus Christ.

This would get both marks. It defines the concept and then develops it.

(b) questions

For these questions you will be expected to describe a religious teaching, belief, idea, practice, place, event or view.

b Describe the teaching of the Catholic Church on the sanctity of life. (5)

Catholics believe each person is unique because God made them. The creation of humans was unlike the rest of creation because they were made in a unique way and in the Image of God. In the first account of Creation in Genesis God makes humans different from all of the other animals. Humans are made in the image of God. The Latin term for in the image of God is imago Dei. This is also mentioned by Saint Catherine of Sienna. The Catholic Church teaches that all human life is sacred and that everyone has a right to life which should be protected and valued at every stage. This means Catholics do not support abortion and euthanasia.

For high marks you should be able to show your knowledge using religious terms and relevant sources of wisdom.

Activity

Look at the sample answer the student has given.

a Use a highlighter to identity the religious language the student has used.
b Underline the two sources of wisdom and authority the student has referred to.

(c) questions

You will be expected to explain a key teaching, belief, idea, practise, event or view.

To gain full marks in this component you will need to:

- Give two religious views. This can be either Catholic Christianity or Judaism, or from Catholicism and another Christian tradition.
- Use appropriate religious terms and any relevant sources of wisdom and authority.
- Remember non-religious views aren't needed in these questions.

c Explain from two different religions or two religious beliefs about the Trinity. (8)

Here are some points you could include in your answer:

Catholic view	Jewish view
Catholics believe in one single God, who made himself known to the world as three distinct Persons. Catholics believe that the Trinity works as one. Yet within this common purpose, each of the three Persons has a special role: • God the Father created heaven and earth • God the Son, Jesus, is the saviour of the world • God the Holy Spirit is an invisible spiritual power which guides, helps and inspires human beings. Without a doctrine of the Trinity, it would not be possible for Christians to believe that Jesus is God. The way the Trinity works is considered to be a mystery, but it does help in understanding some of the qualities of God.	Jews would agree with Catholics that there is one God. The belief in only one God is stated in the Shema. It is also stated in the Ten Commandments. However, they do not accept Jesus as the Son of God or the idea of the Trinity. There are different attributes of God such as 'judge' and creator' but these are only characteristics of the one God.

Activity

1 Give two sources of wisdom and authority you could use in an answer to this question.
2 Use your answer to 1) and the points in the table to write a full answer to this question.

(d) questions

As these questions are worth 15 marks they are really important.

The question requires you to:

- Read and understand the statement.
- Discuss the statement presenting more than one point of view. They don't need to be contrasting views (they can be) but must be different.
- Analyse, evaluate, reach a supported judgement.

In Theme 1 you are required to respond from non-religious viewpoints as well. This is the only question that demands this.

d 'The world is ours to do what we like with.' Discuss this statement showing that you have considered more than one point of view. (15)
(You must refer to religious and non-religious beliefs such as those held by Humanists and Atheists, in your answer.)

Catholics believe that we should care for the planet for God. This is because they believe that God 'appointed man as ruler over all creation' and that it is their duty to care for the earth (for God).

However, Humanists believe that humans should care for the earth for themselves to make us happier. Like Catholics, Humanists do believe in preserving the planet, just not for a God but for future generations.

Pope Francis' 'Laudato Si' says that we should stop treating the earth as we do because we should be stewards of the earth and care for God's creation responsibly. It also says that we should not treat the earth's resources as profit and that we should be grateful for what God left here for us.

Humanists believe that we should preserve the earth and protect it for future generations and to make sure they have a good quality of life so that they can enjoy their time on the earth as much as possible.

Activity

Have a look at the mark bands on pages ix and x. What band do you think the answer falls in?

How might the student improve the answer? Consider:

- sources of wisdom and authority
- religious language
- making a judgement.

Exam practice

a What do Catholics mean by Incarnation? (2)
b Describe the teaching of the Catholic Church on the sanctity of life. (5)
b Describe the teaching of the Catholic Church on the origins of the universe. (5)
b Describe the teaching of the Catholic Church on the origin of evil. (5)
c Explain from two Christian traditions or Catholic Christianity and Judaism, attitudes towards abortion. (8)
c Explain from two Christian traditions or Catholic Christianity and Judaism, attitudes towards the creation account in Genesis. (8)
d 'God is the only explanation for the creation of the universe.' Discuss this statement showing that you have considered more than one point of view. (You must refer to religious and non-religious beliefs such as those held by Humanists and Atheists, in your answer.) (15)
d 'There is no value to suffering.' Discuss this statement showing that you have considered more than one point of view. (15)
d 'Jesus' moral teachings are not relevant for today.' Discuss this statement showing that you have considered more than one point of view. (15)

Death and the afterlife

Key concepts

Death is the end of physical life. When the physical body ceases completely to function.

Eternal life is the term used to refer to life in heaven after death. Also, it is the phrase Jesus uses to describe a state of living as God intends, which leads to a life in heaven.

Catholic teachings on the meaning of death and dying well

REVISED

Catholics believe that **death** is not the end of our existence. Jesus taught that those who believe in him would have **eternal life**; they would go on to live with God after death. This belief should affect how Catholics live their lives – it gives purpose and meaning to their existence. It affects how they should treat those who are dying and approach death themselves. Death should not be seen as the end of life, just a way into a new form of life.

Catholics should prepare themselves to die well. This may include seeking opportunities to spend time with family and make their peace with them. They might want to make sure that they have made arrangements for wills and what will happen when they die. This might include what they would like their funeral to be like.

For those in pain 'preparing for death' will include seeking palliative care to reduce that pain in the final stages of life.

The liturgies and rites of the Church provide comfort for the dying and those who have lost loved ones. Prayers are said for those who have died. Belief in eternal life is explored through music and art.

Catholic teaching on assisted suicide and euthanasia

The Catholic Church rejects **euthanasia** or **assisted suicide** as appropriate ways of ending a life. This teaching is based on the belief that all human life is sacred. Life is a gift from God and so should be respected from conception to natural death. Euthanasia and assisted suicide, are seen as going against that sanctify of life and against the instruction in the Ten Commandments – 'Do not murder.'

Instead they promote the work of hospices and other organisations that provide **palliative care** when treatment to cure a medical condition is no longer possible.

Euthanasia means a 'good' or 'gentle' death. This is where a medical professional gives medication to end the life of a person with a serious illness who is suffering unbearable pain.

Assisted suicide is the term used when an individual seeks help to end their own life in a pain-free way. Some countries have changed their laws to permit assisted suicide.

Palliative care is care for those who are terminally ill and their families.

The importance of palliative care

Hospices, and those organisations that offer similar care, are guided by doctors to provide pain-relieving medication, nursing care, supervision and practical help until natural death occurs. The Catholic Church, along with many other Christians, supports those who provide palliative care because it respects the value of every person until their natural death. Medication is provided to reduce pain and to enable the individual to retain as much dignity and quality of life as possible.

Now test yourself

1. Explain why the Church believes assisted suicide and euthanasia are wrong.
2. Describe how Catholics should prepare for death.

TESTED

Contrasting views on the quality and sanctity of life

REVISED

Sanctity of life is the principle that life is sacred and should not be ended.

Quality of life is the general well-being of a person.

The right to die

People who suffer from incurable diseases might choose to end their life before their illness reaches the final stages. It means that they can choose to control the disease or illness before it becomes too painful. They wish to end their life before their **quality of life** is diminished. A person who is fully conscious and rational has the freedom to choose when to end their life.

Sanctity of life

Catholics believe that all human life is sacred and holy. Life is a gift from God; it is precious and should be respected from conception to natural death. Euthanasia and assisted suicide are going against that **sanctity of life**. It is against the instruction in the Ten Commandments – 'Do not murder.' Anyone who assists in euthanasia is in effect co-operating with murder.

People should be allowed to die with dignity using good palliative care. Hospices offer support and care. It is acceptable to turn off a life support machine if the medical evidence shows the patient is braindead. It is also acceptable for a person to refuse treatment which would prolong a painful illness if the result is out of proportion to the burdens of the treatment, for example, it prolongs their pain and the gain is very limited.

However, it would not be acceptable to withdraw food and fluids to someone in a permanent vegetative state. Giving food and water, by natural or artificial means, is a basic requirement of human dignity. This prevents death by starvation or dehydration.

Quality of life

Some argue that quality of life is more important that whether it is considered special or sacred. If a person is free from pain and lives with dignity, they can be said to have a good quality of life. If they are in constant pain, which is more than any pleasure they might have, they can be said to have a poor quality of life. Some would argue that if a person has a poor quality of life they have a right to die. However, there are problems with measuring quality of life as it is very subjective.

Contrasting views on the right to die argument

For Quality of life arguments	Against Sanctity of life arguments
• Many think it is a basic human right to have control about ending your life. • Advances in medicine have led to people being kept alive who would have previously died. These people should have the right to a painless death. • Those who believe in free will think it is ethically wrong to keep someone alive who has no hope of recovery. • The teaching of Jesus on loving your neighbour can be used to justify assisted suicide, because it might be the most loving thing to do. • We do not let animals suffer so why humans? • People have a right to refuse medical treatment, so why not a right to ask for euthanasia? • People with terminal illnesses want to control when they die so that they can die with dignity.	• Life is created by God and so it is up to God and not humans when people die. • If Euthanasia is legalised the impetus to research into terminal illness is reduced. • People may actually want to live, but may go through with euthanasia because they feel like they are a burden on society. • Accepting euthanasia is a slippery slope. It is a short step from voluntary to compulsory euthanasia. • The role of doctors is to support life and not to destroy it. Would patients trust their doctors? • People might change their minds about wanting to die, but then it would be too late. • All life is special and should be worthy of protection.

Now test yourself

TESTED

1 What is the meaning of 'sanctity of life'?
2 What is the meaning of 'quality of life'?
3 Explain the difference between sanctity and quality of life.
4 Copy and complete the table below, outlining three arguments for and against the right to die.

	For	Against
Argument 1		
Argument 2		
Argument 3		

Catholic beliefs about life after death

REVISED

Catholic beliefs about life after death are summed up in the Nicene creed, which teaches that Jesus rose from the dead and there will be life after death. St Paul explains what will happen after death in his first letter to the Corinthians.

Catholic belief in resurrection of the body (1 Corinthians 15)

In 1 Corinthians, Paul teaches that Jesus rose from the dead and that what happened to Jesus will also happen to his followers. Resurrection is the belief that after death people will have a bodily existence. Paul teaches that people will have a resurrection like Jesus, and will have a spiritual resurrection body given to them by God. This will be a glorified body. When Jesus rose, his body was familiar but at times his disciples did not recognise him.

Sources of wisdom and authority

Now if Christ is preached as raised from the dead, how can some of you say that there is no resurrection of the dead? But if there is no resurrection of the dead, then Christ has not been raised; if Christ has not been raised, then our preaching is in vain and your faith is in vain.

(1 Corinthians 15:12–14)

For I delivered to you as of first importance what I also received, that Christ died for our sins in accordance with the scriptures, that he was buried, that he was raised on the third day in accordance with the scriptures, and that he appeared to Cephas, then to the twelve. Then he appeared to more than five hundred brethren at one time, most of whom are still alive, though some have fallen asleep. Then he appeared to James, then to all the apostles. Last of all, as to one untimely born, he appeared also to me.

(1 Corinthians 15:3–8)

So is it with the resurrection of the dead. What is sown is perishable, what is raised is imperishable. It is sown in dishonour, it is raised in glory. It is sown in weakness, it is raised in power. It is sown a physical body, it is raised a spiritual body. If there is a physical body, there is also a spiritual body.'

(1 Corinthians 15:42–44)

Now test yourself

TESTED

1 Describe in your own words what St Paul says about the resurrection of Jesus. What will this be like for everyone else?

Popular beliefs about survival of the soul

REVISED

- Christianity, Judaism and Islam believe in the existence of a **soul**. The soul is the spiritual part or essence of a person. It is non-physical and lives on after death.
- Most Christians believe in the immortality of the soul. They believe that when the body dies, the soul leaves the body to live with God. The soul is the essence of a person and at death it leaves the body. It is eternal and continues to live on to everlasting life in heaven.
- Other Christians say the body and soul are one and cannot be separated. After death the soul is temporarily apart from the body, but body and soul will be reunited on Judgement Day. At the **resurrection** we will rise bodily from the dead, just as Jesus rose from the dead.

Key concepts

The **soul** is the eternal part of a human being given at conception, which lives on after the death of the body. Also a name for a human being's rational nature – their mind.

Resurrection is the raising of the body to life again after death. Christians believe that Jesus has already experienced resurrection and that all people will experience it at the end of time.

Contrasting views about death as the end of personal existence

REVISED

- Most Humanists and Atheists are materialists. In this view, nothing else exists apart from matter or material. Humans are just a physical body. This means that there is no soul, we are just made of matter. There is no spiritual aspect to life. This is the only life we have and therefore should make the most of it. There is no life after death.
- Some people believe in reincarnation. Sikhs and Hindus believe that at death the soul passes to a new body. How you are reborn depends on good or bad actions in this life. People are reborn countless times in many different ways.

Now test yourself

TESTED

1. What is the meaning of the term 'resurrection'?
2. How is 'resurrection' different from 'survival of the soul'?
3. What might a Humanist say about life after death?

Eschatology

Key concepts

Judgement is when each individual will be held to account by God for the things they have done or failed to do during their lives.

Heaven is for those who have accepted God's grace and forgiveness in this life; they will enjoy an eternal existence in God's presence in the next life. This face-to-face encounter with God is what is called 'heaven'.

Hell is for those who through the exercise of their own free will ultimately reject God's grace and forgiveness; they will have chosen to live eternally outside of God's presence. This total lack of God for all eternity is what is called 'hell'.

Catholic teaching on heaven and hell

REVISED ☐

In Christianity, eschatology is the study of what happens at the 'end times' or the 'end of the world'. The Catholic Church's teaching about life after death is summarised in the four last things: death, **judgement**, **heaven** and **hell**. When a person dies they are judged by God and this decides if they go to heaven or hell.

The parables of judgement

Catholics believe that when a person dies, God passes judgement on his or her soul. This is called 'particular judgement'. Each person is responsible for their own actions. There will be a final judgment when the whole of creation will be judged. This idea is found in the parable of the sheep and the goats (Matt 25:31–36).

Heaven

Christians believe that a person who has lived a holy life will be rewarded with eternal happiness in heaven. Heaven is to be at one with God. In the Bible, heaven is often described as a banquet or a feast, but Christian ideas about it vary widely. The Bible teaches that there is no sadness, pain or suffering in heaven. Christians take this to mean that heaven is a holy, happy and peaceful state of being with God. Christians agree that it is difficult to accurately describe what it is like, since it is beyond human experience.

Hell

Christianity teaches that hell is a place or state of being where unrepentant sinners go after death. An unrepentant sinner is someone who does not regret the things they have done wrong and refuses God's offer of forgiveness and salvation through Jesus. A well-known image of hell, as an underground place of eternal fire and suffering, is based on images in the Bible. Most Christians believe that hell is a place of suffering and of eternal separation from God. The punishment takes the form of spiritual desolation or isolation from God.

Many people have a problem with the idea that an all-loving God would allow people to go to hell. However, Christians believe that God is just and fair, and so cannot let evil go unpunished.

Catholic teaching on purgatory

REVISED

All Christians agree that the world to come after death will be very different from the life we live now. Therefore, those who have died need to be prepared for the change. They need to transfer from the sinfulness of this world to the purity of the next. Catholics believe in a state before heaven that is called purgatory. It comes from the word 'purge', to cleanse or get rid of sin. They think that most people are not bad enough to go to hell but not good enough to go straight to heaven, as they have sinned in their lives on earth. Purgatory is a state of purifying, a time of cleansing and preparation to enter heaven. St Paul used the image of fire in his first letter to the Corinthians, 'It will be revealed with fire, and the fire will test the quality of each person's work. If what has been built survives, the builder will receive a reward.' (1 Cor 3:13) Belief in purgatory is shared by the Orthodox Churches. Protestant Christians do not accept this idea of purgatory.

Catholics believe that they can help the souls in purgatory by praying for them. There is a long tradition of praying for the dead. Catholics can ask God for mercy to forgive the soul's sins so that they can enter heaven.

Sources of wisdom and authority

Matthew 18:21–35 'The parable of the unforgiving servant'

- Jesus tells of a man who owes money to the king.
- Not wanting to go to prison, he begs the king for mercy.
- After receiving mercy and being free from his debt, the man goes in search of a man who owes him money.
- This other man asks him for mercy, however, he rejects the requests for mercy.
- The king is furious and puts the first man in prison until he pays what he owes.
- Jesus finishes the story with these words: 'So also my heavenly Father will do to every one of you, if you do not forgive your brother from your heart.' (Matthew 18:35)

Luke 16:19–31 'The rich man and Lazarus'

- A rich man lives a life of luxury but ignores Lazarus, the beggar who lives at his gate.
- Lazarus dies and is taken to heaven. At the same time the rich man dies and is taken to hell.
- The rich man asks for some comfort, but he is reminded: 'Son, remember that you in your lifetime received your good things, and Lazarus in like manner evil things; but now he is comforted here, and you are in anguish.' (Luke 16:25)
- The message of the story is that everyone will be judged on how they have lived their life and rewarded accordingly.

Now test yourself

TESTED

1 Describe what the scripture passages Matthew 18:21–35 and Luke 16:19–31 reveal about the nature of the afterlife.
2 Explain what Christians believe about the soul.
3 Explain what Catholics believe about life after death.

The Magisterium

Key concept

The **Magisterium** is the teaching authority of the Church, exercised by the bishops in communion with the Pope. In exercising magisterium, the Church is given grace by the Holy Spirit to faithfully interpret the scriptures and tradition.

Popes and bishops

REVISED

In the Catholic Church, there are several figures and groups of people who are also believed to be sources of authority.

- **Pope** – leads the Church. Every Pope is the successor of St Peter. This means he does the same job Peter once did. What Jesus said to Peter applies to his successors too.
- **Cardinals** – a small group of senior clergy, some in charge of dioceses, others assisting the Pope. Their best-known function is to elect a new Pope.
- **Archbishops** – senior bishops.
- **Bishops** – are responsible for a diocese and all the priests within it. They give the sacrament of Holy Orders.
- **Priests** – are responsible for the spiritual care of a parish and celebrate the sacraments. Some priests belongs to religious orders (for example Jesuits, Benedictines) and specialise in prayer, preaching or teaching.
- **Laity** – these are the body of the faithful, those who are not clergy.

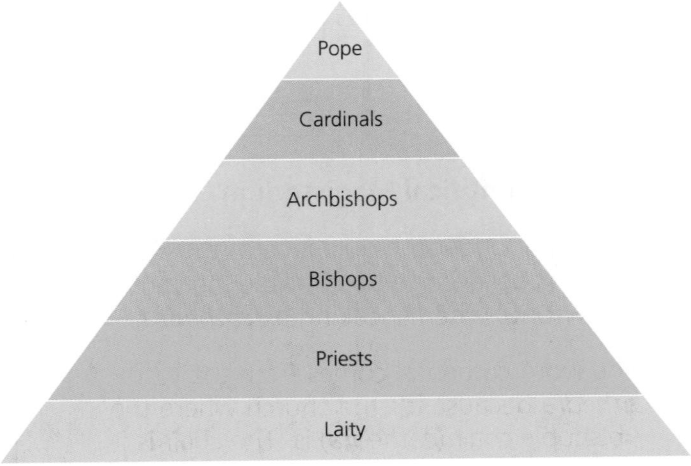

Pope
Cardinals
Archbishops
Bishops
Priests
Laity

The Magisterium

REVISED

The Latin word **magisterium** means 'teaching authority'.

- The Pope and the bishops safeguard the Church's teaching on behalf of everyone.
- It is the responsibility of the Pope and the bishops to ensure that the teachings of Jesus are protected.
- They also have the authority to make decisions and statements about faith and morality for the Catholic community. The Magisterium can address issues that are not mentioned in the Bible, for example it can give guidance on things like same-sex partnerships, contraception, ecology and nuclear weapons.
- Catholics believe the Holy Spirit guides the Pope and bishops in their decisions.
- As the Pope is guided by the Holy Spirit, Catholics believe he is infallible. This means he cannot make a mistake when teaching definitively about matters of faith that the Catholic Church believes should be held by all Christians.

Magisterium can be exercised in two ways: Ordinary Magisterium and Extraordinary Magisterium.

Ordinary Magisterium

This is the everyday teaching of the Church.

- Bishops regularly preach **homilies** and write letters to their diocese encouraging Catholics in their faith and giving them instruction.
- The Pope may write a letter known as an encyclical. These letters are addressed to the world on contemporary issues to reinforce, reiterate, or re-state Church teaching. The name of each letter consists of the first two words of the letter in Latin, the language it is written in. For example, Pope Francis issued *Laudato si*, which is about how we should care for the environment. This means that Catholics should listen to the Pope and take their part in looking after the planet.

Extraordinary Magisterium

Extraordinary Magisterium

These are times when the teaching authority of the Church is used but they don't happen very often.

This comes about in two ways:

Pontifical Magisterium

The Pope, under the guidance of the Holy Spirit, is believed to be infallible (he can't be wrong) when speaking ***ex cathedra***.

The word cathedral comes from the Latin *cathedra* because it's the church where the bishop's chair (*cathedra*) is. The chair is symbolic of authority. In practice, popes very rarely use their authority in this way.

The most recent pronouncements made under the infallible teaching authority of the Pope are the dogmas of the Immaculate Conception and the Assumption of the Blessed Virgin Mary.

Conciliar Magisterium

This is when the Pope calls together all the bishops to settle a problem or explore new questions facing the Church.

There have only been 21 councils.

The climax of these councils is a written letter that explains the faith, interprets Scripture, or settles disputed topics of faith and morals.

The ecumenical councils have defined doctrines such as the divinity of Christ (Nicaea). The last council was Vatican II held in the 1960s.

Now test yourself

TESTED

1. Describe what is meant by 'Magisterium'.
2. Explain in your own words the difference between Ordinary and Extraordinary Magisterium.
3. Explain whether you think Magisterium is needed today.

Ecumenical council is a gathering of Church leaders to discuss matters of faith.

A **homily** is a short talk given by a priest explaining the readings of the day.

Ex cathedra comes from the Latin phrase 'from the chair'. It refers to the Pope's authority on matters of faith and morals.

The Second Vatican Council (Vatican II)

History and importance

The 1960s was a time of dramatic change around the world. The Second Vatican Council was an **ecumenical council** of the Catholic Church during which bishops from all over the world came together to discuss how Catholicism needed to meet the challenges of the modern world.

The Council took place between 1962 and 1965. It was started by Pope John XXIII who died in 1963 and it was completed by Pope Paul V.

Four key documents of the Second Vatican Council

REVISED

Gaudium et spes (the Pastoral Constitution on the Church in the Modern World)	*Sacrosantum concilium* (the Constitution on the Sacred Liturgy)
This is a document about Catholic social teaching. This encouraged Catholics to respond to the issues of poverty and social justice, the impact of science and technology. It encourages people of faith to engage with the modern world.	This document covers changes to the Church's official public worship. Before the Council Mass was said in Latin and everyone faced the altar. So the words were translated into the local language and the altar was moved so that the priest now faces the people and their actions are more easily seen. In addition, the lectionary (the collection of Bible passages read at Mass) was revised so that Catholics get a richer and wider selection of Bible readings.
Dei verbum **(the Dogmatic Constitution on the Word of God)**	***Lumen gentium*** **(The Dogmatic Constitution on the Church)**
This document sets out how important the Bible is. It encouraged Catholics to use the Bible as part of their prayers. It has led to an increase in specialist biblical scholars and more Bible study groups in parishes.	*Lumen gentium* means 'the light of the peoples' and this document encouraged ordinary Catholics to take a more active role to be part of the mission of the Church and to serve Jesus. This means that all Catholics should act on the promise they made at their baptism to be 'lights to the world' by being of service to others.

Changes brought about by Vatican II

REVISED

Before the Council	After Vatican II
Mass was said in Latin.	Mass now said in the vernacular (local language) so people can understand what is said.
The priest and congregation faced the altar to show the link between the Eucharist and Jesus' sacrifice.	The altar turned around and the priest faces the people so everyone can see. Increases sense of community and participation.
The priest leads everything.	Lay people are encouraged to read and be Eucharistic minsters. More women get involved.
The congregation only receive communion in the form of bread.	Communion under both bread and wine encouraged.
Bible reading did not play a big part in the lives of many Catholics.	More emphasis on the Liturgy of the Word. Catholics encouraged to read scripture.
Catholics encouraged to see themselves as different from other Christians and not to mix with them. Catholics were not allowed to go to Protestant churches.	Emphasis placed on what all Christians believe in common. Catholics encouraged to work for Christian Unity and pray with other Christians. This is called ecumenism.
Closed off to other religions and cautious of world views.	Open to dialogue with people of other faiths especially Judaism. Catholics encouraged to see Jews as brothers and sister, because Christians share with Jews a special relationship with God that is called the covenant.

Now test yourself

TESTED

1. When asked why the Second Vatican Council was needed, Pope John reportedly opened a window and said, 'I want to throw open the windows of the Church so that we can see out and the people can see in.' Explain how this statement reflects the purpose of the Council.
2. List five key differences in the Catholic Church before and after the Council.
3. Explain the purpose of each of the four main documents of Vatican II.

Artefacts

From very early on in the history of Christianity believers have expressed their faith through objects, from the decorations carved into sarcophagi through to the lighting of the paschal candle at Easter.

Sarcophagi

REVISED

In Rome it was custom for wealthy people to be buried in stone tombs called **sarcophagi**. They were usually decorated with scenes from mythology and with Roman gods. The first Christians adapted this practice; they continued to use the stone tombs but developed images that would reflect their beliefs about eternal life.

A **sarcophagus** is a stone coffin.

Sarcophagus with scenes of Jesus' passion

One example is the sarcophagus with scenes of Jesus' passion that is now in the Pio Cristiano Museum in the Vatican, Rome. It dates from the fourth century and has a variety of images that reinforce the belief that Jesus' death and resurrection was a triumph over sin, and a sign of hope. The entire decoration is based on the Passion and Resurrection of Jesus. In the Early Christian period, when believers were working out ways of visually showing their religion, they relied on the example of art around them and biblical stories.

- On one panel, there is an illustration of the scene where Simon of Cyrene was helping to carry Jesus' cross to the crucifixion.
- The next panel shows Jesus being given a crown of thorns by the soldiers guarding him; they gave him the crown to mock him as he was accused of calling himself king of the Jews. However, the crown in the image is actually filled with jewels which symbolises that Jesus' death was actually a triumph over sin.
- Another panel shows Jesus being presented for trial before the Roman governor, Pilate.
- The next panel is the scene of Pilate, who did not want to execute Jesus but gave in to the pressure of the crowd and the Jewish authorities, washing his hands to symbolise that he wouldn't take responsibility for crucifying Jesus.
- Christ is not shown here hanging on the cross. The early Christians did not depict Jesus either as dead or in suffering. Instead, at the centre there is a stylised cross with the 'Chi-Rho' symbol standing for Jesus. The Chi-Rho is an ancient symbol of the resurrection. It is formed from the first two letters of the title 'Christ' in Greek (Chi is X, Rho is P), merged together they form the Chi-Rho.
- The Chi-Rho is placed within a wreath that is held in the beaks of two eagles. The wreath is the Roman symbol of victory. The eagles represent God because in Roman religion they were used to represent the God Jupiter. This shows the fact that Jesus' death was a victory over sin and death.
- This cross sits above two soldiers who are looking up at it in wonder. It expresses the hope that what happened to Jesus will also happen to those who believe in him.

Now test yourself

TESTED

1 What is the meaning of the term 'sarcophagus'?
2 What is the meaning of the term 'Chi-Rho'?
3 Describe the scenes depicted on the sarcophagus at the Pio Cristiano Museum.
4 Copy and complete the table below, explaining how the illustrations and symbols found on the sarcophagus express Catholic belief about eternal life.

Illustration or symbol	Catholic belief about eternal life
Crown of thorns	
Pilate washing his hands	
The symbol of the Chi-Rho	
The wreath	
The two eagles	
The two soldiers	

The paschal candle

REVISED

The paschal candle is a candle used during Easter week in the church; it symbolises the fact that Jesus' resurrection was a triumph over death.

The Easter Vigil

The paschal candle is lit at the Easter Vigil, in remembrance of the resurrection.

- At the beginning of the Easter Vigil the church is in darkness.
- Outside the church a fire is lit.
- The Easter (paschal) candle is lit from that fire and processed into the church.
- The candle is raised three times with the chant 'The light of Christ' and the people respond, 'Thanks be to God.'
- This symbolises that 'light of Christ' overcoming the 'darkness of sin'.
- The procession is completed with an ancient hymn, called the 'Exultet', which proclaims Christ's triumph over sin because his resurrection defeats death.

The Easter candle has a prominent place in the church throughout the whole Easter season. As a reminder of the triumph of the resurrection the Easter candle is lit at every Mass from Easter Sunday through to Pentecost. It is used in church over the Easter period and then throughout the year.

The symbols on the candle

The Paschal calendar represents Jesus' light overcoming sin and death. It is decorated with symbols to show this.

- The 'alpha' and 'omega': these are the first and last letters in the Greek alphabet. They symbolise Christ as the 'first' and the 'last'; the 'beginning of all things' and the 'end of all things'.
- The cross: this is the symbol of Christian faith because it is due to the crucifixion of Christ that the resurrection was possible.
- The five wounds: the candle has five studs on it to represent the five wounds Jesus received during his crucifixion.
- The year: each year the candle is marked with that particular year. It reminds people that Jesus is the same for all time and that the salvation earned by Jesus is as real now as it was in the past.

Use of the Easter candle in baptisms

- The Easter candle is used in baptisms throughout the year. To remind the people of the resurrection, it is lit and placed near to the font. A smaller baptismal candle is lit from its flame and is given to the baptised person or their family to remind them that the 'Light of Christ' has defeated the darkness of sin.

As well as at baptisms, the Easter candle is also used at funerals; it is placed near the coffin to signify the hope of the resurrection.

Now test yourself

TESTED

1 Copy and complete the table below, explaining the meaning of the symbols found on the paschal candle.

Symbol	Meaning
The 'alpha' and 'omega'	
The cross	
The five wounds	
The year	

2 Under what circumstances might Catholics use the paschal candle?

Answers at www.hoddereducation.co.uk/myrevisionnotes

Music and the funeral rite

The significance of different forms of music in worship

REVISED

Singing and music has been a part of Christian worship since the earliest days of the Church. As Christianity has its roots in Judaism it continued to use the Book of Psalms for its prayers. The **psalms** are poetic and were written to be sung. They continue to be used today in worship, but they also became the model for Christian **hymns**.

A hymn is a type of religious song, written for worship or prayer. Christian hymns are often written with special or seasonal themes and these are used on holy days such as Christmas, Easter or during particular seasons such as Advent and Lent. Hymns with a Christmas theme are known as carols.

Others are used to encourage reverence for the Bible or to celebrate Christian practices such as the Eucharist or baptism. Some hymns praise or address individual saints, particularly the Virgin Mary; such hymns are very common in Catholicism.

Music for the Mass

The main form of Catholic worship is the Mass. Music is an important part of Mass. Most Masses will include hymns, probably at the beginning and ending with one. It is also likely that there will be a hymn at the offertory, when the bread and wine are taken up, and during communion. The hymns used will probably be based on the readings for the day or be influenced by the liturgical year. For example, you would expect hymns in Easter to reflect the joy of the resurrection as that is what Catholics are celebrating then.

However, Catholics are encouraged to sing the parts of the Mass itself. The parts of the Mass that are generally repeated in each liturgy are:

1. Kyrie ('Lord have mercy')
2. Gloria ('Glory be to God on high')
3. Credo ('I believe in one God'), the Nicene Creed
4. Sanctus ('Holy, Holy, Holy')
5. Agnus Dei ('Lamb of God')

Latin is the language of the Catholic Church, but nowadays these responses are often in English. There are different settings for these responses.

How music expresses Catholic beliefs about eternal life: Fauré's *Requiem*

The **Requiem** Mass is a modified version of the ordinary Mass, which is said at a Catholic funeral. Musical settings of the Requiem Mass have a long tradition in Western music. There are many examples, but one of the most famous is by Gabriel Fauré (1845–1924). Fauré attempts to convey Catholic beliefs about eternal life in his music. In his *Requiem* he wanted to show that you could be sad about the death of loved ones while also hoping that after death they had gone on to eternal life with God. Fauré said that he did not want to express a fear of death. Instead the requiem focuses on the hope that the dead will be in heaven. He expresses this in the music using harps, violins and the sound of angelic sopranos. Fauré's music helps the grieving to have faith, comfort and hope. It does not focus on sadness, but on the peaceful and fear-free nature of death. The music brings a sense of calm and peace.

A **hymn** is a type of religious song, written for worship or prayer.

A **psalm** is a prayer song or hymn, particularly from the Book of Psalms. Used in Jewish and Christian worship.

Requiem comes from the Latin word for rest. It refers to a Mass for the dead.

Now test yourself

TESTED

1. What is the meaning of the term 'hymn'?
2. Why might Catholics wish to sing the parts of the Mass instead of singing hymns?
3. Explain how Fauré's *Requiem* expresses Christian belief about life after death.

Catholic funeral rites

REVISED

Catholics believe that death is not the end. As Christians, they can look forward to eternal life with God in heaven.

At a Catholic funeral, the mourners pray for the person who has died, entrusting them to the love of God. They believe that God listens to their prayers and will be merciful towards the departed person.

The service is also a celebration of a life. The mourners look back over the dead person's life and thank God for the good times they enjoyed.

The symbols, prayers and texts of the Catholic funeral rite in Britain

A Catholic funeral usually takes place as part of a form of liturgical worship known as a Requiem Mass (Requiem for short). Requiem means 'rest' in Latin and it reflects the fact that Catholics are praying that the person who has died is now at peace with God.

- The coffin may be brought to the church the night before the funeral. The priest meets the procession of the coffin and the mourners at the church door. The coffin is sprinkled with holy water as a reminder of the dead person's baptism and the promise of sharing in Jesus' resurrection.
- The coffin is usually put near the altar. The priest places a book of the gospels and a crucifix on it. The gospels signify the person's life dedicated to the teachings of Jesus, and the crucifix reminds believers that in baptism the deceased received the sign of the cross and will share in Jesus' victory over sin and death.
- Mass is celebrated with readings and prayers focused on the Christian hope of eternal life. After the Liturgy of the Word comes the homily, when the priest explains the meaning of the readings. The homily normally includes a tribute to the person who has died. The priest will focus on the belief that those who trust in God and Jesus will go on to eternal life.
- The funeral ends with burial or cremation. For a cremation, the coffin is taken to the crematorium and there is a short committal service. For a burial, the body is taken to the churchyard or cemetery and lowered into the grave. The prayers for the committal are said. Relatives and friends throw handfuls of earth into the grave, showing that they are sharing in laying their loved one to rest.
- The funeral is usually followed by a reception at the family's home or another location where food and drink are served.

Now test yourself

TESTED

1. How does a Requiem express Catholic belief about life after death? (You may find it useful to refer back to the section on life after death when answering this question.)
2. Describe the main sequence of events at a Requiem Mass.
3. Explain how the Requiem Mass reflects Catholic beliefs about life after death.

Prayer within Catholic communities

The significance of prayer

REVISED

The *Catechism of the Catholic Church* defines prayer as 'raising the mind and heart to God'. This means being totally focused on God.

For Catholics, prayer is communicating with God. Catholics pray together through liturgical worship, most commonly the Mass. This is normally called public worship. Catholics also pray on their own, this is called private prayer or private worship.

Catholics can use formulaic prayers. These are prayers which have been passed down over many years as part of the Church tradition, for example, the Lord's Prayer (Our Father, Glory Be and Hail Mary).

Or they might use their own words to speak to God. This is called extempore prayer. It is more spontaneous and does not require planning or preparation. What matters is that Catholics make prayer a part of their life to build their relationship with God.

The Lord's Prayer

Jesus taught his disciples to pray using the Lord's Prayer or Our Father. It is a model for prayer because it contains Adoration, Thanksgiving, Confession and Supplication (ACTS).

- **A**doration means worship. Catholics are encouraged to begin their prayer by praising God for who he is and for all that he has done.
- **C**onfession (repentance) means telling God about the things that you have done wrong. They ask God to forgive them.
- **T**hanksgiving means being thankful to God.
- **S**upplication, petition or intercession, means praying for their own needs and for the needs of others.

Sources of authority and wisdom

Our Father, who art in heaven, hallowed be thy name; thy kingdom come, thy will be done on earth as it is in heaven. Give us this day our daily bread; and forgive us our trespasses as we forgive those who trespass against us; and lead us not into temptation, but deliver us from evil. Amen.

('Our Father' or 'Lord's Prayer')

Views on prayer

Prayer is not asking. Prayer is putting oneself in the hands of God, at his disposition, and listening to his voice in the depth of our hearts. (Mother Teresa)

But when you pray, go into your room and shut the door and pray to your Father who is in secret; and your Father who sees in secret will reward you. (Matthew 6:6)

Ask, and it will be given you; seek, and you will find; knock, and it will be opened to you. For every one who asks receives, and he who seeks finds, and to him who knocks it will be opened. (Matthew 7:7–8)

Praying for and offering Masses for the dead

REVISED

Catholics have a long tradition of praying for the dead.

- They ask God to welcome the deceased into his presence so they can have eternal life in heaven. The most commonly used prayer is: 'Eternal rest grant unto him/her, O Lord. Let perpetual light shine upon him/her. May he/she rest in peace. Amen.'
- A Catholic might ask a priest to offer a Mass for a relative or friend who has died. The person's name may be mentioned during the Eucharistic prayer.

Now test yourself

TESTED

1. What is the meaning of 'prayer'?
2. Explain the importance of prayer for Catholics.
3. Explain why Catholics dedicate prayers or offer Masses for loved ones who have died.

Knowledge check

Question a) is always about definitions of key concepts. Make sure you know them.
Use the look, cover, write and check technique to learn them. Look at the concept. Cover it and then write it down. Finally check your answer.

Death	The end of physical life. When the physical body ceases completely to function.
Eternal Life	The term used to refer to life in heaven after death. Also, the phrase Jesus uses to describe a state of living as God intends which leads to this life in heaven.
Heaven	Those who have accepted God's grace and forgiveness in this life will enjoy an eternal existence in God's presence in the next life. This face to face encounter with God is what we call 'Heaven'.
Hell	Those who through the exercise of their own free will ultimately reject God's grace and forgiveness, will have chosen to live eternally outside of God's presence. This total lack of God for all eternity is what we call 'Hell'.
Judgement	Judgement is when each individual will be held to account by God for the things they have done or failed to do during their lives.
Magisterium	The teaching authority of the Church, exercised by the bishops in communion with the Pope. In exercising the Magisterium, the Church is given grace by the Holy Spirit to faithfully interpret the scriptures and tradition.
Resurrection	The raising of the body to life again after death. Christians believe that Jesus has already experienced resurrection and that all people will experience it at the end of time.
Soul	The eternal part of a human being given at conception which lives on after the death of the body. Also a name for a human being's rational nature – their mind.

Summary questions

1 What is euthanasia?
2 What is palliative care?
3 Explain the term 'sanctity of life'.
4 What is the right to die?
5 What is eschatology?
6 What is resurrection?
7 What is the soul?
8 Explain what is meant by heaven, hell and purgatory.
9 What is Magisterium?
10 What does *ex cathedra* mean?
11 Give an example of Ordinary Magisterium.
12 What is a sarcophagus?
13 What does Requiem mean?
14 What is a paschal candle?
15 What is prayer?
16 What is the point of praying for someone who is dead?

Crime and punishment

Key concepts

Sin is acting against the will or laws of God.

Absolutism is the belief that there are certain actions that are always right or always wrong. The belief that moral laws exist eternally and are not just human inventions.

Relativism is the belief that there is no moral law and that rules that govern what is right and wrong are human inventions and change from place to place and from age to age.

Crime and sin

REVISED

What is a crime?

- When someone breaks the law they commit a crime.
- Laws are there to show what acceptable behaviour is so that people can live safely and without fear.
- Laws are made by the government and can vary from country to country. For example, in some states of America you need to be 21 to buy alcohol, whereas in Britain it is 18.
- What is lawful can change over time, for example homosexuality was illegal in this country but is not anymore.

What is a sin?

- A **sin** is an action which goes against the will or laws of God.
- Some sins are crimes, for example murder and stealing. Other sins such as adultery and pride are not against the law.

Making moral decisions

REVISED

Sin and crime are concerned with our behaviour. Deciding what is right or wrong is known as morality. Making decisions on how we should behave can be complex; very simply there are two common forms of morality.

Absolute morality

- This is when a person has a principle such as 'stealing is wrong'. This applies in all situations, no matter what the context or circumstance.
- For example, stealing is always wrong. It would be wrong for me to steal food, even if my family where starving. Another example would be the belief that it is wrong to directly and intentionally take innocent life. This would apply in all situations, including abortion and euthanasia. There is no circumstance where it is acceptable. Taking a life in self-defence or in defence of one's society, for example, in war, is not an exception to this absolute moral principle.

Relative morality

- This is the idea that a moral principle can be adapted or adjusted in certain situations.
- So stealing in principle is wrong, but if I have no other way to get food then stealing is acceptable. I might think killing is wrong, but if I need to defend myself then it might be reasonable to do so.

Now test yourself

TESTED

1 Explain, with the use of examples, the difference between sin and crime.
2 Explain, with the use of examples, what is meant by 'relative' and 'absolute' morality.

Aims (rationales) of punishment

REVISED

When a criminal is found guilty of a crime, there are a number of **punishment** options available to a judge, such as prison, fines and community service. A judge will consider the advantages and drawbacks of several different purposes when sentencing a person for the crime they have committed.

Key concept

Punishment the consequences of a wrong decision and a penalty imposed by a person in authority on the person who has committed wrong-doing.

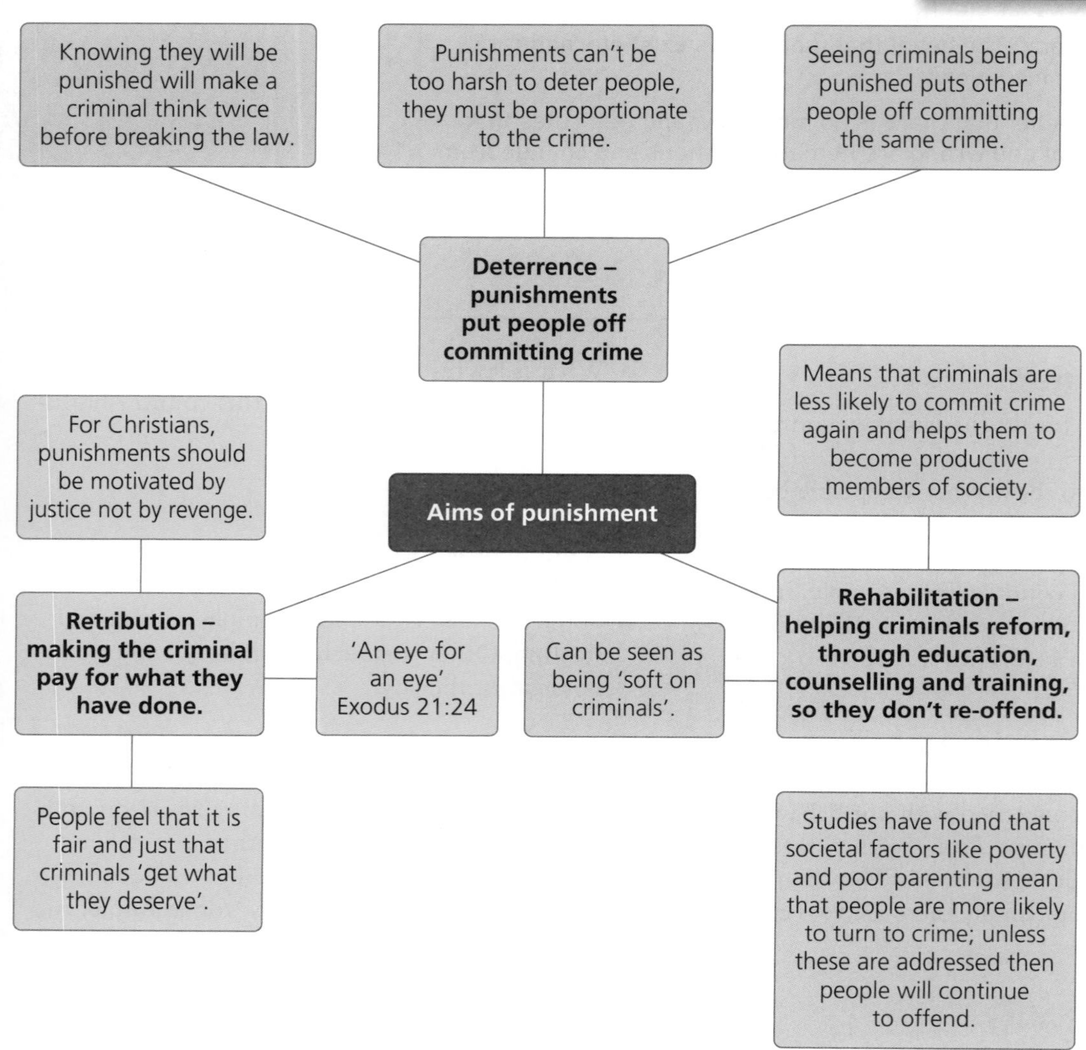

Now test yourself

TESTED

1 Draw a Venn diagram like the one on the right. Add examples of:
   a sins that are not crimes
   b crimes that are not sins
   c sins that are also crimes.

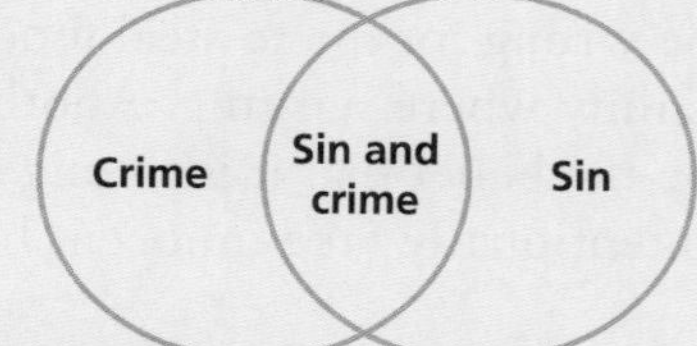

2 Copy and complete the table below for each of the three aims of punishment.

Aim of punishment	Strength	Weakness
Deterrence		
Retribution		
Rehabilitation		

Christian teachings about forgiveness

REVISED

Key concept

Forgiveness is the act of pardoning someone for the offences they have caused you, of overlooking a person's faults.

Forgiveness is at the heart of the Gospel message. Jesus' example and teaching shows Christians that they should treat others with compassion, love, mercy and forgiveness.

- In Matthew 18:21–22, the Parable of the unforgiving servant, Jesus makes it clear that there is no limit to forgiveness.
- The importance of forgiveness is emphasised in the Lord's Prayer. Christians ask God to 'forgive their sins, as they forgive those who have sinned against them'. This means Christians can only expect to receive forgiveness from God if they are forgiving towards others.
- There are many examples from Jesus' life for Christians to follow:
  - Jesus forgave the woman caught in adultery John 8:1–11 telling her to 'go and sin no more'.
  - He visited Zacchaeus the tax collector, a known cheat, allowing him to change and reform.
  - The parable of the prodigal son is one of Jesus' best-known stories. Some think it should be called the parable of the forgiving father because the father forgives his son and welcomes him back even though he had done wrong.
  - Jesus showed forgiveness in the last moments of his life as he was being put to death. While he was on the cross he says, 'Father, forgive them for they do not know what they are doing.'

Sources of wisdom and authority

Then Peter came to Jesus and asked, 'Lord, how many times shall I forgive my brother or sister who sins against me? Up to seven times?' Jesus answered, 'I tell you, not seven times, but seventy-seven times.

(Matthew 18:21–22, The parable of the unforgiving servant)

For if you forgive other people when they sin against you, your heavenly Father will also forgive you. But if you do not forgive others their sins, your Father will not forgive your sins.

(Matthew 6: 14–15)

What do these two quotes tell Catholics about how they should forgive?

Is forgiveness just letting people off?

REVISED

In the Bible, there is a tension between forgiveness and punishment. As well as teaching about forgiveness Jesus also spoke about justice. He also spoke about God's punishment for wrong-doers, in the next life. On judgement day, God will judge all humans according to how they have behaved. If they have behaved justly they will be rewarded in heaven.

It is up to God to judge people and he will forgive those who are truly sorry for what they have done and want to change.

Many Christians believe that punishment and forgiveness can go together. Many Christians would see the main role of punishment as being to help the person involved to reform.

Now test yourself

TESTED

1 What is meant by 'forgiveness'?
2 How did Jesus show forgiveness in his life?

Catholic teaching on capital punishment

REVISED

Capital punishment is also known as the death penalty. It means a person is put to death or executed as a punishment for their crime. It was abolished in the United Kingdom in 1965, but it is still legal in many countries. Whether it is ever justifiable is a controversial topic.

Some people think it is a good form of punishment because it deters people from murdering others and takes a life for a life. Other people disagree with capital punishment because evidence shows it does not deter, and innocent people can be killed for crimes they did not commit.

Development of catholic teaching on capital punishment

The *Catechism of the Catholic Church* states: 'Assuming that the guilty party's identity and responsibility have been fully determined, the traditional teaching of the Church does not exclude recourse to the death penalty.' (*Catechism of the Catholic Church*, 2267)

Traditionally the Catholic Church has allowed, but not encouraged capital punishment. The Catholic position on capital punishment has developed over many years.

In two famous letters (see Sources of wisdom and authority box, right), St Augustine emphasises the need to seek other punishments if at all possible. Pope John Paul II in *Evangelium Vitae* 56, suggested that capital punishment should be avoided unless it is the only way to defend society from the offender: In any event, the principle set forth in the new *Catechism of the Catholic Church* remains valid: 'If bloodless means are sufficient to defend human lives against an aggressor and to protect public order and the safety of persons, public authority must limit itself to such means, because they better correspond to the concrete conditions of the common good and are more in conformity to the dignity of the human person.'

Recently Pope Francis has stated that he is against the death penalty, saying that it is no longer justifiable and there is also the possibility that the wrong person might be killed.

Sources of wisdom and authority

Whoever sheds human blood, by humans shall their blood be shed; for in the image of God has God made mankind.

(Genesis 9:6)

... eye for eye, tooth for tooth, hand for hand, foot for foot ...

(Exodus 21:24)

You have heard that it was said, 'Eye for eye, and tooth for tooth.' But I tell you, do not resist an evil person. If anyone slaps you on the right cheek, turn to them the other cheek also.

(Matthew 5:38–39)

Sources of wisdom and authority

...we pity the person, but hate the offence or transgression. In fact, the more we dislike the vice in question, the less do we want the offender to die without correcting his vices [...] There is no space to reform character except in this life.

(Letter 153 to Macedonius, 3)

...we would prefer to have them set free than to have the sufferings of our brothers avenged by shedding their blood.

(Letter 134 to Apringius, 4)

What do these two texts from Augustine tell us about capital punishment?

Now test yourself

TESTED

1 What is the meaning of the term 'capital punishment'?
2 Describe the Catholic view of capital punishment.

Arguments for capital punishment	Arguments against capital punishment
1 Jesus never taught the death penalty was wrong.	**1** Jesus came to save (reform) sinners, but you cannot reform a dead person.
2 The Old Testament teaches that the death penalty should be used for some crimes.	**2** The fifth Commandment says, 'Do not kill.'
3 Some Christians would argue that the death penalty upholds the commandment 'thou shalt not kill' by showing the seriousness of murder as a crime.	**3** Jesus said that revenge is wrong. Matthew 5:38 'You have heard that it was said, 'Eye for eye, and tooth for tooth.' But I tell you, do not resist an evil person. If anyone slaps you on the right cheek, turn to them the other cheek also.'
4 St Paul teaches that Christians should accept and obey the laws of their country, which might include the death penalty.	**4** Christianity teaches that all life is sacred, if abortion and euthanasia are wrong so is capital punishment. Only God has the right to give and take away life.
5 The Catholic Church has not cancelled their statements that capital punishment can be used by the state.	**5** The overall message of Christianity is love and forgiveness so capital punishment goes against this.
	6 There is always a risk that the wrong person might be killed.
	7 Saint Augustine says we should try to use other forms of punishment if possible.

Non-religious views on capital punishment

Arguments for capital punishment	Arguments against capital punishment
Retribution is a major part of punishment and the only retribution for murder is the death penalty.	No court can be sure that the correct verdict is given – wrongly accused prisoners can be released but not if they've been executed.
Human life is the most important thing there is and the value will only be shown by giving those who take human life the worst possible punishment.	Statistics show that countries without the death penalty have lower murder rates than those who have it.
It acts as a good deterrent.	Murderers regard life imprisonment worse than death.

Now test yourself

TESTED

1 Read the three sources of wisdom, then match each source to the viewpoint it supports:

Source of wisdom	Viewpoint
Genesis 9:6	If someone kills someone then it is fair that they should be killed – so capital punishment is justified.
Exodus 21:24	Capital punishment is wrong because Jesus taught that we should respond peacefully even if someone is violent towards us.
Matthew 5:38–39	Capital punishment is wrong because all life is sacred.

2 'Catholics shouldn't support capital punishment.' Plan a response to this statement showing that you have considered more than one point of view. Aim to:

a Include both sides of the argument.

b List two or more arguments in favour and against.

c Include at least one quote to back up each point of view.

Redemption

Key concept

Salvation is the belief that through Jesus' death and resurrection humanity has achieved the possibility of life forever with God.

The meaning and significance of salvation for Catholics

REVISED

Catholics believe that **salvation** is part of God's plan. Humans turned their back on God by sinning. This 'original sin' was committed by Adam and Eve as recorded in Genesis 3. This brought the need for salvation. Every human since then has been part of a broken relationship with God.

The *Catechism of the Catholic Church* says that Jesus offers salvation, 'that human beings are saved by Jesus' life on earth, his death, resurrection and ascension. [Jesus] accomplished this work [of salvation] principally by the **paschal mystery** of his blessed **passion**, **resurrection** from the dead and glorious Ascension, whereby 'dying he destroyed our death, rising he restored our life'.' (*Catechism of the Catholic Church*, 1067)

Christians believe that:

- Humans rejected God by their sins; humans are so important to God that God sent Jesus to free humans from the effects of sinfulness.
- Their relationship with God depends on Jesus' life, death and resurrection. Without it, they cannot be close to God or obtain forgiveness of their sins.
- They need to repent of their sins, asking God for forgiveness, and accept Jesus Christ as the Son of God and saviour of the world.

Paschal mystery is the suffering, death and resurrection of Jesus.

Resurrection refers to Jesus rising from the dead.

Redemption is the forgiveness of sins through Jesus' sacrifice; redemption is part of salvation.

Passion refers to Jesus' arrest, trial and suffering.

The role of grace in redemption

REVISED

Grace is the love and mercy shown by God because God wants people to have it, not because they have done anything to deserve or earn it. It is a free and undeserved gift from God. Jesus is the saviour of the world for Christians. Christians believe they do not deserve this but are given it freely by God. They must accept this freely in faith.

The life, death, resurrection and ascension of Jesus

REVISED

The life of Jesus

During his life Jesus showed people what God is like and how to live. For example:

- He taught us that God is a loving father.
- Love is at the heart of the Gospel message.
- God has a special place for the poor and needy, 'The first will be last and the last will be first.'
- Jesus showed God's care by forgiving sins and healing the sick.
- Jesus spent his life with the poor and needy.

The death of Jesus

The gospels record that after the Last Supper, Jesus went with his disciples to a garden called Gethsemane, he was arrested there after one of his disciples, Judas, told the authorities where to find him.

Jesus was tried by the Sanhedrin (the Jewish religious leaders). He was found guilty of blasphemy, the crime of either insulting God or pretending to be God. The punishment for blasphemy was death. Pontius Pilate, the Roman in charge of the city of Jerusalem, sentenced Jesus to be whipped and crucified. Roman soldiers then mocked and beat Jesus before leading him away to be crucified.

Jesus' death is often explained using the idea of **sacrifice**:

- In the Bible, animal sacrifice was common.
- The person making the sacrifice hopes to mend a relationship with God.
- The animal was seen as taking the blame for something it did not do, and the sacrifice was believed to free human beings from the sins they had committed.
- Jesus' total obedience to God was so powerful that it made up for the sins of human beings in a way that other sacrifices could not.

Sacrifice means to make an offering of yourself or a gift at a big cost.

The resurrection

The resurrection is the central belief of Christianity and lies at the heart of the Christian faith. The gospels record that after Jesus died on the cross, his body was buried, but he rose from the dead three days later.

- Catholics believe Jesus overcoming death proves he was the Son of God. Only God can conquer death.
- The resurrection demonstrates that Jesus is their saviour.

The ascension

The gospels' account of Jesus' ascension tells how he was taken up into heaven 40 days after his resurrection. The significance of the ascension for Catholics is:

- Jesus' mission on the earth was complete.
- He had completed everything God the Father had intended him to do.
- Jesus returns to heaven to prepare a place for his followers.
- Jesus' ascension prepared the way for the Holy Spirit to come to earth, as he had promised at the Last Supper.

Now test yourself

TESTED

1. Explain how Catholics believe the life, death, resurrection and ascension of Jesus saves them.
2. Explain why Catholics believe salvation is necessary.
3. Describe two ways the resurrection is significant for Catholics today.

A loving God's mercy

REVISED

Some people might ask the question 'a loving God would want to save everyone. He would not want to condemn anyone to hell.'

- Humans have free will and must choose how to spend their life.
- If a person chooses to do evil, then they will be far from God no matter how much God wants them to come to him.
- God's love is unconditional but he cannot force it upon us, we have to accept it.
- The idea of free will means that God can only offer salvation: it is up to the individual to accept that offer.

Church

The Church: the people of God

REVISED

In Greek, *ecclesia* is the word for church. It means assembly, or gathering together, the assembly of God's people. The Church is the people of God gathered together. The word church with a small 'c' is used to refer to the building where Christians come to pray. When it is written with a capital 'C', Catholics mean everyone who is a member of the Church, all believers gathered together. The Church is an important idea to Catholics.

The nature of the Church: the four marks

REVISED

<table>
<tr><th colspan="2">The four marks of the Church</th></tr>
<tr><td colspan="2">At the Councils of Nicaea and Constantinople in the fourth century CE, Church leaders agreed upon a single statement of faith called the Nicene Creed. It identifies four marks, or distinguishing qualities of the Church: one, holy, catholic and apostolic.</td></tr>
<tr><th>One</th><th>Holy</th></tr>
<tr><td>The Church is one. The Catechism notes that the Church is one for three reasons:
● because of its source, which is the Holy Trinity, a perfect unity of three divine persons, Father, Son and Holy Spirit
● because of its founder, Jesus Christ, who came to reconcile and unite all mankind through his death on the cross, taking away their sins
● because of its 'soul', the Holy Spirit, who dwells in the souls of the faithful, who unites all of the faithful into one communion of believers, and who guides the Church.
The Church is united in the Body of Christ.</td><td>The Church is also holy. Catholics believe Jesus is the source of all holiness. Jesus makes the Church holy and uses it to make people holy. It does this through its teaching, prayer and worship, and good works, making the Church a visible sign of holiness.</td></tr>
<tr><th>Catholic</th><th>Apostolic</th></tr>
<tr><td>The Church is catholic. Saint Ignatius of Antioch used this word, meaning 'universal' or 'whole', to describe the Church. The Church has the task of reaching out to the whole world with the message of Jesus. The Church is for everyone.</td><td>Finally, the Church is apostolic. Catholics believe that Jesus Christ founded the Church and gave his authority to his apostles. He entrusted a special authority to St Peter, the first Pope and Bishop of Rome, to act as his representative on earth. The Church is also apostolic in that the faith was preserved, taught and handed on by the apostles.</td></tr>
</table>

Mary as a model of the Church

REVISED

Catholics hold Mary in great honour. She was chosen to be the human mother of God the Son, Jesus Christ, and you will often hear her described as Mary, Mother of God. Without Mary, there would be no Jesus, no Incarnation and therefore no salvation.

Mary is often called 'Our Lady' by Catholics. This is a special title given to no one else, showing how special she is. All Catholic churches will have a statue of Mary and there is a special devotion to her.

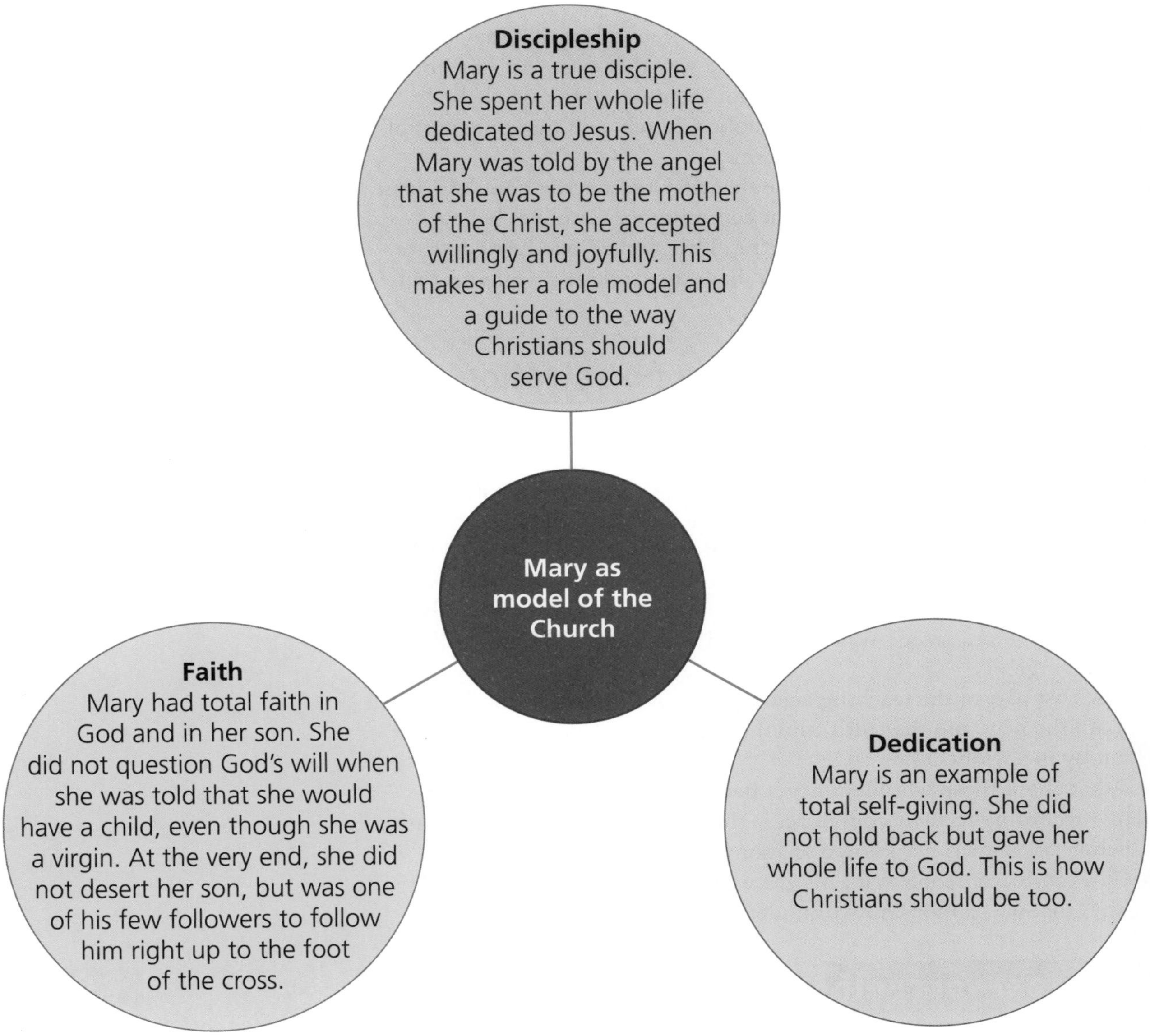

Mary as model of the Church

Discipleship
Mary is a true disciple. She spent her whole life dedicated to Jesus. When Mary was told by the angel that she was to be the mother of the Christ, she accepted willingly and joyfully. This makes her a role model and a guide to the way Christians should serve God.

Faith
Mary had total faith in God and in her son. She did not question God's will when she was told that she would have a child, even though she was a virgin. At the very end, she did not desert her son, but was one of his few followers to follow him right up to the foot of the cross.

Dedication
Mary is an example of total self-giving. She did not hold back but gave her whole life to God. This is how Christians should be too.

Now test yourself

TESTED

1 Describe the four marks of the Church.
2 Explain why Mary is a model of the Church.

The Church as body of Christ

REVISED

In the New Testament, the Church is described as 'the body of Christ' especially by Saint Paul in his first letter to the Corinthians (1 Corinthians 12:27). As Catholics consider themselves to be the physical form of Jesus on earth (the Body of Christ), they must continue with his physical work, ministering help and teaching. For Catholics, this also shows that Jesus is still active in the world. His work didn't end with his death, but it continues in those that follow and believe in him.

- Jesus lives on through his followers, and in the Church, which is his body on Earth.
- Each person within the Church has a different talent that they can use for the good of the Church in the same way that each part of a body has a different function and is used for the good of the whole body.
- Christians become part of the Catholic Church, and therefore part of the Body of Christ, through baptism.
- At the Eucharist Catholics believe that they receive the body of Christ. By sharing the consecrated host at communion, Catholics believe that they share in the body of Christ. They are fed by Christ and are strengthened. Coming together to share the Eucharist reaffirms their unity.

'Outside the Church there is no salvation'

REVISED

A very old, traditional saying of the early Church fathers was: 'Outside the Church there is no salvation' (*Catechism of the Catholic Church,* 845–846). This claim does not mean that Protestants, non-Catholic Christians, non-Christians and Atheists or agnostics are not saved. This claim is not telling us that Catholics are in Heaven and everyone else is in Hell. Rather it is an answer to the question of a sincere person who wants to know, 'Has God acted in the world to provide some way for me to be holy and therefore saved? Where do I find what I need to become holy, more loving?'

- The first part of the teaching echoes Jesus' own words in John's Gospel: 'I am the way, and the truth, and the life; no one comes to the Father, but by me.' (John 14:6)
- What about those who have never heard the Gospel? As long as they live according to their conscience – they may achieve salvation. These people are sometimes known as anonymous Christians.
- God can reach people with his grace to bring salvation to all people in ways that we cannot know or understand.

Now test yourself

TESTED

1 Explain how Catholics understand the concept of the body of Christ.

'Christ has no body now on earth but yours, no hands but yours, no feet but yours, yours are the eyes through which Christ's compassion is to look out to the earth, yours are the feet by which He is to go about doing good and yours are the hands by which He is to bless us now.' (St Teresa of Avila)

2 Explain how Saint Teresa's prayer can help us to understand why Christians are part of the body of Christ.

3 Pope Francis has said that God will 'forgive' Atheists as long as they behave morally and live according to their consciences. Explain this using the idea of 'outside the Church there is no salvation'.

Buildings

A Catholic church is the place of worship where Catholics gather as a community to celebrate their faith. The most common form of worship is Mass or the **Eucharist**. Most Catholics will attend a local parish church.

The orientation of Catholic churches

REVISED

Traditionally, churches face towards the east. Another word for east is 'orient'. This is where we get the word orientating from. For the first Christians, it was customary to pray facing toward the Holy Land, where Jesus was born, lived, died and rose again. Also the sun rises in the east and is a reminder of the resurrection of Jesus bringing new life.

Key concepts

Eucharist means 'thanksgiving'. It is the name Catholics use to describe the rite where the bread and wine become the body and blood of Jesus and are received by the people. Also the name for the real presence of Jesus in the sacrament of Holy Communion.

Sources of wisdom and authority

A church, 'a house of prayer in which the Eucharist is celebrated and reserved, where the faithful assemble [...] ought to be in good taste and a worthy place for prayer and sacred ceremonial.

(*Catechism of the Catholic Church*, 1181)

Architectural features of Catholic churches: how they facilitate worship and reflect the mystery of salvation

REVISED

- Towers and steeples represent prayer and worship rising up to heaven, a sign of what takes place inside the building.
- Churches are often very tall with domes or vaulted ceilings. This creates a space which is pointing up, showing a connection with God and heaven.
- It is also common for churches to be cruciform (cross-shaped). This is to signify the importance of the death of Jesus.
- Modern church buildings tend to be simpler in design. As a result of Vatican II and the changes it made to worship, some churches built since the 1960s are radically different. For example, some churches are circular in design with the altar in the middle. This signifies the oneness of the worshippers and that they are all sharing in the sacrificial meal at the altar. It can also stand for the eternity of God.
- Very often stained glass is used in churches. The windows usually display stories from the Bible or lives of the saints.

How the sacred objects within a church represent Catholic beliefs about salvation

REVISED

Whatever the design, the whole church will be focused on the sanctuary. Sanctuary means holy place. This is where the altar, lectern and tabernacle are. The sanctuary is where the public worship is focused. These are features you'd always expect to find in a Catholic church.

The altar

The altar is a table structure, which is usually made out of stone. The main action of the Mass, the liturgy of the Eucharist, takes place at the altar. The priest consecrates bread and wine here. 'Altar' reminds Christians of the sacrifice and death of Jesus on the cross. Jesus offers salvation and redemption from sin. The altar is also a table, reminding Catholics that they are sharing in a fellowship meal, as they recall the meal Jesus shared with his disciples at the Last Supper. For Catholics, the sacrament of the Eucharist or Mass is one of the most important sacraments. On or near the altar are candles, representing the Christian belief that Jesus is the light of the world.

Lectern

Near the altar is a book stand which is called a lectern or ambo. It is from here that the priest, deacon or reader reads from. At the Liturgy of the Word scripture is read from here. Catholics believe that at Mass they are nourished and fed by listening to the word of God. At services, they will read from a lectionary. A lectionary is a book containing a collection of scripture readings appointed to use on a given day.

The baptismal font

The baptismal font is a big stone bowl filled with water where baptism takes place. Baptism is the first sacrament by which a person becomes a Christian. It used to be by the main door to the church to show that people entered the Church through baptism. Now the font tends to be at the front so that all those present can easily see a baptism when it takes place.

The tabernacle

A tabernacle is a safe-like place in which the consecrated host are kept. The sacrament is reserved here so that it can be taken to the sick and those who are unable to come to church. It is also a focus for private prayer and devotion. Catholics will genuflect, go down on one knee, towards the tabernacle in honour of the presence of Jesus reserved in the Blessed Sacrament. The tabernacle is often behind the altar, but in some modern churches it is sometimes placed in a side chapel so that people can pray in private. A sanctuary lamp is found nearby, which reminds Catholics of the presence of God in the tabernacle.

The crucifix

In Catholic churches there is always a crucifix, a cross with an image of the crucified Christ on it. It is usually on or near the altar. It serves as a reminder of the suffering and death of Jesus. Catholics believe that the death of Jesus was the price he paid for their salvation. Catholics, like all Christians, believe that Jesus died for them to forgive their sins and give them eternal life.

Other sacred objects

As people come into the church they pass a holy water container or stoup. They sign themselves with water, making the sign of the cross to remind themselves of the Trinity, the death of Jesus and their own baptism. It also helps to focus their mind into a reverent attitude as they enter the church.

Other important features of a Catholic church are Stations of the Cross. They are especially used in Lent to focus worship on the death of Jesus.

Statues are usually found around the church to help people pray. One of them will usually be of Our Lady. In front of the statue there will probably be votive candles. In Catholic churches, Christians place a lighted candle symbolising their prayer.

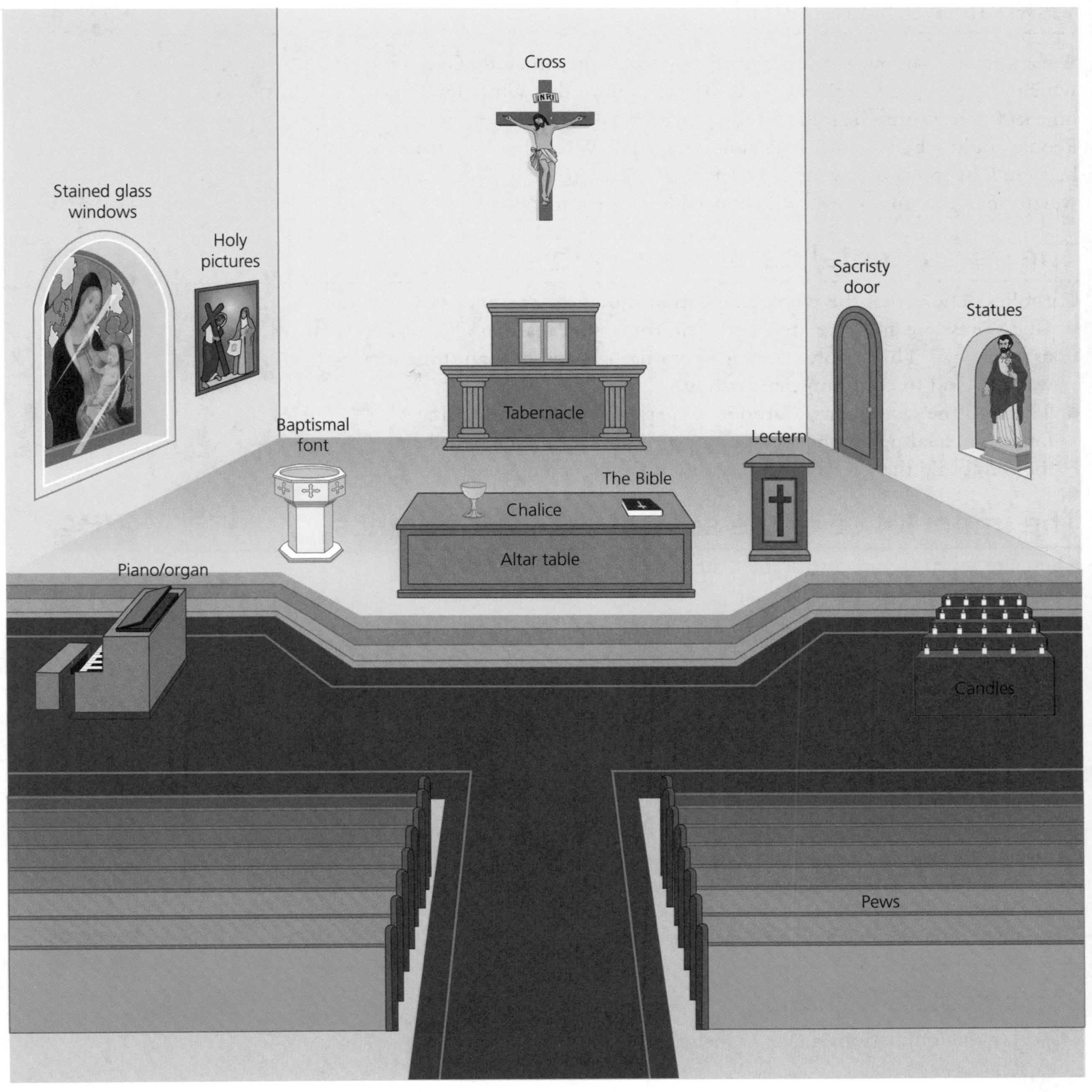

Now test yourself

TESTED

1. Why do churches face east?
2. Choose three examples of architectural features of a Catholic church, and explain how each one either facilitates worship or reflects the mystery of salvation.
3. Choose three examples of sacred objects from inside a Catholic church, and explain how each one represents Catholic beliefs about salvation.

Sacraments

What is a sacrament?

REVISED

A sacrament is 'an outward sign of inward grace, ordained by God, by which grace is given to the soul.' Catholics believe that while Jesus was on earth, everything he said and did was a visible sign of God's love. People could see him, hear him and touch him. When Jesus returned to heaven, Christians believe that he left the Church to be his body, and the way to see, hear and touch him is through the sacraments.

The sacramental nature of reality

REVISED

Catholics believe that the whole of creation shows the presence of God:

- God's presence and love are not distant things but realities all around us every day. This involves seeing every natural and human thing as a way for God to communicate with us.
- Through the sacraments, Catholics experience God's nourishing, forgiving, healing, strengthening power in a special way. This helps them to build their relationship with God and become more like Jesus.

The importance of the sacraments to Catholics

REVISED

There are seven sacraments in the Catholic Church:

1. Baptism
2. Confirmation
3. Eucharist
4. Penance
5. Anointing of the sick
6. Holy orders
7. Matrimony

These sacraments originated in the life, work and teachings of Jesus. To Catholics, the sacraments are a meeting point with God. Each one builds up an individual's relationship with God in a different way.

The seven sacraments

REVISED

Sacraments of initiation

These lay the foundation of every Christian life.

Baptism

For Catholics, baptism is the first step in a lifelong journey of commitment and discipleship. At the service of baptism, water is poured on a baby's head while the priest or deacon says, 'I baptise you in the name of the Father, and of the Son and of the Holy Spirit.'

Meaning and significance

The person being baptised becomes part of the family of God. Baptism takes away original sin and gives a new birth in the Holy Spirit. Its sign is the pouring of water.

Catholic families are encouraged to baptise their children soon after birth, however sometimes people are baptised later, or even as adults.

Confirmation

As most Catholics are baptised as babies, confirmation is done when they are older. It is usually given by the bishop. Its signs are the laying-on of hands on a person's head and anointing with oil.

Meaning and significance

Confirmation completes the sacrament of baptism. If baptism is the sacrament of re-birth to a new life, confirmation is the sacrament of maturity and coming of age. It gives the strength to follow Jesus and to become involved in the mission he left to the Church.

Eucharist

At the Last Supper, Jesus took bread and wine and asked his followers to re-enact the meal when they come together. Its signs are the bread and wine that Catholics receive at Mass – the body and blood of Christ.

Meaning and significance

Catholics believe the Eucharist, or Communion, is both a sacrifice and a meal. They believe in the real presence of Jesus, who died for humanity's sins. As they receive his body and blood, they are fed spiritually.

Sacraments of healing

These celebrate the healing power of Jesus.

Penance (confession)

The signs of this sacrament are the confession of sins and the priest's words of absolution.

Meaning and significance

By expressing sorrow for their sins in the sacrament of penance or reconciliation, Catholics experience God's forgiveness and healing. Their relationship with God and their unity as a Church is made whole again.

Anointing of the sick

The individual is anointed with oil (a symbol of strength) and receives the laying-on of hands from a priest.

Meaning and significance

This unites a sick person's suffering with that of Jesus and brings forgiveness of sins. It brings strength in illness, comfort from suffering, and prepares those close to death to meet God.

Sacraments at the service of Communion

These help individuals to serve the community and bring about the salvation of others.

Holy orders

The signs of this sacrament are the laying-on of hands and anointing with oil by a bishop.

Meaning and significance

In holy orders, men are ordained as priests, deacons, or bishops. Priests serve as spiritual leaders of their communities. When ordained people follow Christ in their ministry of service, they act in the place of Christ. This is one of the ways God's presence is made known for their community.

Matrimony

The couple give the sacrament to each other and their wedding rings and vows are the signs of this sacrament.

Meaning and significance

In matrimony, or marriage, a baptised man and woman are united as a sign of the unity between Jesus and his Church. God is present through the couple's lifelong love and commitment to each other.

The importance of the Mass for Catholics

REVISED

The Mass or Eucharist is the liturgical service where Catholics gather to recall the Last Supper, when Jesus took bread and wine and asked his disciples to remember him when they did the same. For Catholics, it is the most regularly celebrated sacrament. Mass is celebrated every day of the year except Good Friday and Easter Saturday. Catholics should attend Mass on Sunday and as often as they can.

Mass is said to be 'the source and summit of the Christian life', because being unified with God is the most important thing to Catholics. It is at the heart of their spiritual life; they become closer to God because they receive Jesus in communion.

- Mass re-enacts the sacrifice of Jesus on the cross, so it is the highest form of prayer that a believer can make.
- By receiving the Eucharist in Communion, Christ's body and blood spiritually feeds the believer.
- It makes individual Catholics part of the body of Jesus or the Church.

Catholics believe that Christ is present in the Mass:

- in the consecrated bread and wine, which are Jesus' body and blood
- in the readings, since Jesus is the word of God and the readings, especially the gospel
- in the believers gathered together
- in the person of the priest (Catholics believe that Christ works through the ministry of the priesthood to transform the bread and wine into his body and blood).

Now test yourself

TESTED

1 What is meant by a sacrament?
2 Copy and complete the following table, explaining the signs, effects and significance of each of each of the seven sacraments.

Sacrament	Sign	Effects	Significance
Baptism			
Confirmation			
Eucharist			
Penance			
Anointing of the sick			
Holy orders			
Matrimony			

3 Explain why Mass is so important to Catholics?

Mission and evangelisation in Britain and elsewhere

Key concept

Evangelisation literally means spreading the 'good news' which we translate as gospel. The sharing of the gospel and life of Jesus with others.

Catholic teaching on evangelisation

REVISED

Jesus sent his apostles out into the world on a mission to 'make disciples of all nations, baptising them in the name of the Father and of the Son and of the Holy Spirit' (Matthew 28:19–20). All Christians are called to continue this work of announcing the gospel. Missionaries have travelled the world to share the gospel.

No longer is **evangelisation** focused on places where the gospel has not been heard before. Now the largely secular West is also a place where the gospel message needs to be heard.

Evangelisation doesn't mean forcing people to convert. It is about sharing and living out the message. When a person has heard the gospel it is their own personal choice what to do next.

Evangelii gaudium

REVISED

In 2013, Pope Francis wrote a letter to the world on the theme of the Church's mission of evangelisation in the modern world. It is called *Evangelii gaudium*, which in Latin means 'The joy of the gospel.' Pope Francis says the way to share the gospel is to show love and care for the weak, vulnerable and poor.

He wants 'a Church which is poor and for the poor' (*Evangelii gaudium* 198), and for the Church to have a special love and care for 'above all the poor and the sick, those who are usually despised and overlooked.'

The Pope says:

- Catholics must care for 'the homeless, the addicted, refugees, indigenous peoples, the elderly who are increasingly isolated and abandoned, and many others.'
- Parishes should be welcoming places, ready to greet new people and receive them into the community.
- Catholics should be outward looking; this means they should look for new ways to spread the gospel message.

Sources of wisdom and authority

Key points and quotes from *Evangelii gaudium*:

15. '[...] evangelisation is first and foremost about preaching the Gospel to those who do not know Jesus Christ [...] this is the first task of the Church'.

48. 'Who should be first to be evangelised? The Poor and Sick.'

49. 'I prefer a Church which is bruised, hurting and dirty because it has been out on the streets, rather than a Church which is unhealthy from being confined and from clinging to its own security.' This means Catholics should take risks and engage with the world.

197–198. 'God's heart has a special place for the poor, so much so that he himself "became poor" (2 Corinthians 8:9). 'This is why I want a Church which is poor and for the poor.'

264. 'The main reason for evangelisation is to share the love of God.'

Catholic beliefs on the relationship between faith and salvation influence ideas on mission and evangelisation

REVISED

Locally

This basic message of God's love is passed on by the parish (celebration of the Mass, sacraments, Bible study, charitable work, social events, parish retreats, outreach events, etc.). Also the parish can engage with other Christian churches, other faith communities. Individual Catholics might choose a career like teaching, medicine or caring which demonstrates Christ's love for the world. They might work as a catechist, sharing their faith with other people. A catechist is someone who works in the parish preparing people to receive the sacraments. Being married and raising children to follow Jesus is one of the ways Catholics live out the gospel.

How does the Church engage in evangelisation?

Nationally

On a national level, the Bishops' Conference of a country helps Catholics to know and share the gospel. In 2015 a national evangelisation initiative called *Proclaim '15: building missionary parishes,* was introduced by the Church through Cardinal Vincent Nichols: it was designed to affirm the good work that is already being done by the Catholic community, and to provide resources to develop new expressions of Catholic missionary outreach. Individual Catholics might attend national events and conferences to share their faith.

Globally

The Church proclaims the gospel to the whole world through the global figure of the Pope who visits countries representing the Church. He attends World Youth Days. The Church also uses modern media like Twitter and YouTube.

The Church lives out the Gospel in the work of international charities like CAFOD and CARITAS.

Now test yourself

TESTED

1. What is the meaning of the term 'evangelisation'?
2. Describe the key messages of *Evangelii gaudium*.
3. Explain how a Catholic might engage in evangelisation.

Evangelising in Britain: benefits and challenges

REVISED

The UK is a multi-faith society in which people of different religions, and no religion, live alongside each other. According to the 2011 census, the profile of religious belief in Britain has changed. Results of the 2011 census compared to the 2001 census show an increase in the diversity of religious and non-religious beliefs and practices (including those of Christianity, Buddhism, Hinduism, Islam, Judaism, Sikhism, Humanism and Atheism), while also showing that over half of those who responded considered themselves Christian. Britain is now a place which has an increasingly diverse pattern of religious and non-religious beliefs and practices.

This diversity brings benefits and challenges. The Catholic Church teaches that people of other faiths should be respected and Catholics should be sensitive to those who have no beliefs yet seek to do good. Less people are familiar with the gospel story now also less people attend church regularly so it might be difficult to reach people.

Religious diversity

REVISED

RELIGIOUS DIVERSITY

Benefits
- Greater tolerance and understanding of the beliefs of others.
- Varied and rich cultural life from experiencing the religions and traditions of others.
- Better understanding of different viewpoints.
- New ways of living and enjoying life.

Challenges
- It is not always easy to be open and understanding towards the views of others.
- Tensions can exist between different faith groups.
- Some people's beliefs and values may be ignored.
- How can Christians spread the gospel if people aren't interested in it?

Issues
- **Conversion** – there can be issues where one group of religious believers try to convert another, to their faith, which could cause conflict.
- **Interfaith marriages** – when two members of different religions get married. This could cause conflict between families with different beliefs and values.
- **Raising children** – within interfaith marriages both parents might want their children raised within their own faith. This could lead to confusion and arguments.

Interfaith dialogue

Religious leaders are often involved in interfaith dialogue. This is led by the following principles:

- Recognise the common features between faiths
- Respect differences
- Listen to each other
- Learn to live and work in unity
- Share common values such as respect, tolerance, charity and non-violence

Christian traditions, non-Christian and non-religious traditions

REVISED

In the UK laws, festivals and traditions are rooted in the Christian tradition. Two of the main holiday periods in the UK are Christmas and Easter, although it is much more common now to see celebrations of Eid, Diwali and Chinese New Year to name a few.

In recent times we have also seen the emergence of Humanist celebrations of births, weddings and funerals. These occasions have traditionally been linked to a religious celebration but many non-religious people can see the benefit of celebrating these events in an open, honest and sincere way outside of a faith tradition and without the mention of God.

Now test yourself

TESTED

1 Explain the main benefits and challenges of living in a multicultural society.

Knowledge check

Question a) is always about definitions of key concepts. Make sure you know them.
Use the look, cover, write and check technique to learn them. Look at the concept. Cover it and then write it down. Finally check your answer.

Absolutism	The belief that there are certain actions that are always right or always wrong. The belief that moral laws exist eternally and are not just human inventions.
Eucharist	Meaning 'thanksgiving'. The name Catholics use to describe the rite where the bread and wine become the body and blood of Jesus and are received by the people. Also the name for the real presence of Jesus in the sacrament of Holy Communion.
Evangelisation	Literally means spreading the 'good news' which we translate as gospel. The sharing of the gospel and life of Jesus with others.
Forgiveness	The act of pardoning someone for the offences they have caused you. Overlooking a person's faults.
Punishment	The consequences of a wrong decision and a penalty imposed by a person in authority on the person who has committed wrong-doing.
Relativism	The belief that there is no moral law and that rules that govern what is right and wrong are human inventions and change from place to place and from age to age.
Salvation	The belief that through Jesus' death and resurrection humanity has achieved the possibility of life forever with God.
Sin	Acting against the will or laws of God.

Summary questions

1 What is a sin?
2 What is the difference between absolutism and relativism?
3 What is a crime?
4 What do Christians teach about forgiveness?
5 What is capital punishment?
6 What is salvation?
7 What is the paschal candle?
8 Outline how Jesus died.
9 What are the four marks of the Church?
10 What do Catholics call Mary?
11 What is an altar?
12 What is a font for?
13 Why do churches face towards the east?
14 Name the sacraments.
15 Why is Mass important for Catholics?
16 What is evangelisation?

Exam focus

(a) questions

a What do Catholics mean by sin?

A sin is doing something wrong.

(b) questions

b Describe three sacred objects inside a Catholic Church. (5)

A Catholic church is the place Catholics gather to worship. The whole church will be focused on the sanctuary. Sanctuary means holy place. This is where the altar, lectern and tabernacle are. The altar is a table usually made out of stone. The main action of the Mass takes place at the altar. The priest consecrates bread and wine here. For Catholics, the Sacrament of the Eucharist or Mass is one of the most important sacraments. Near the altar is a book stand. It is called a lectern or ambo. It is from here that the priest, deacon or reader reads from. At the Liturgy of the Word scripture is read from here. In Catholic churches there is always a crucifix, a cross with an image of the crucified Christ on it. It is usually on or near the altar. It serves as a reminder of the suffering and death of Jesus. Catholics believe that the death of Jesus was the price he paid for their salvation. Catholics, like all Christians, believe that Jesus died for them to forgive their sins and give them eternal life.

Activity

This is a good answer. Another object the student could have discussed was the font. Add to the answer above showing how the font reflects Catholic beliefs about salvation. Ensure you include specialist language and a source of wisdom and authority.

(c) questions

c Explain how Catholic beliefs about life after death are shown in the funeral rites. (8)

A Catholic funeral usually takes place as part of a form of liturgical worship known as a Requiem Mass (Requiem for short). Requiem means 'rest' in Latin and it reflects the fact that Catholics are praying that the person who has died is now at peace with God.

The coffin is sprinkled with holy water as a reminder of the dead person's baptism and the promise of sharing in Jesus' resurrection. The priest places a book of the gospels and a crucifix on it. The gospels signify the person's life dedicated to the teachings of Jesus, and the crucifix reminds believers that in baptism the deceased received the sign of the cross and will share in Jesus' victory over sin and death.

Mass is celebrated with readings and prayers focused on the Christian hope of eternal life. After the Liturgy of the Word comes the homily, when the priest explains the meaning of the readings. The homily normally includes a tribute to the person who has died. The priest will focus on the belief that those who trust in God and Jesus will go on to eternal life.

The coffin is taken to the churchyard or cemetery and lowered into the grave. The family throw handfuls of earth into the grave, showing that they are sharing in laying their loved one to rest.

(d) questions

d 'Euthanasia should be allowed.' Discuss this statement showing that you have considered more than one point of view. (15)

Activity

Use the framework below to help you structure your response to this question. Remember there is no requirement to include a non-religious belief in your response. However, if the statement lends itself to such a response, feel free to add one.

Agree	Disagree
P make a point	**P** make a point
E explain the point fully (include religious language and teachings)	**E** explain the point fully (include religious language and teachings)
E evaluate the validity or strength of the point	**E** evaluate the validity or strength of the point
P make a point	**P** make a point
E explain the point fully (include religious language and teachings)	**E** explain the point fully (include religious language and teachings)
E evaluate the validity or strength of the point	**E** evaluate the validity or strength of the point

Exam practice

a What do Catholics mean by Eucharist? (2)
b Describe the teaching of the Catholic Church on forgiveness. (5)
b Describe the teaching of the Catholic Church on salvation. (5)
c Explain Catholic beliefs on why Mary is the model of the Church. (8)
c Explain why evangelisation is important to Catholics. (8)
c Explain how a Catholic would view the different aims of punishment. (8)
d 'Capital punishment is just legal murder.' Discuss this statement showing that you have considered more than one point of view. (15)
d 'What Christians believe about life after death is no more than wishful thinking.' Discuss this statement showing that you have considered more than one point of view. (15)

The study of Judaism

Below is a summary of the key questions for this study of Judaism.

- What is the nature of God?
- Why are there different views about the Messiah?
- Why are the covenants with Abraham and Moses so important?
- What's special about the Ten Commandments?
- How do Jews show the importance of *pikuach nefesh* (saving a life)?
- What is the relationship between free will and the *mitzvot*?
- What are the different views about the afterlife?
- What happens in a synagogue?
- Why is the home so important?
- What happens at a bar mitzvah?
- What are the main features of a wedding ceremony?
- What happens when someone dies?
- How does daily life reflect Jewish belief and practice?
- What is the origin, meaning and celebration of Rosh Hashanah, Yom Kippur, Pesach and Sukkot?
- Why are there different views and practices between Orthodox and Reform Jews?

Key concepts

A **synagogue** is a house of assembly; building for Jewish public prayer, study and assembly.

Shekhinah is the place where God's presence rests and can be felt.

Shabbat is the day of spiritual renewal and rest. Beginning at sunset on Friday and closing at nightfall Saturday.

Kosher means 'fit' or 'proper'. Foods that are permitted to be eaten according to Leviticus 11. It is also used to refer to the purity of ritual objects such as Torah scrolls.

Torah is the five books of Moses (Genesis, Exodus, Leviticus, Numbers and Deuteronomy). Regarded as the holiest books of the Tenakh.

Mitzvot is a term that has a mix of meanings. It is often used to refer to duties (such as the 613 in the Torah) and good deeds.

The **Messiah** is the anointed one who some Jews believe will bring in a new era or age for humankind. This will include rebuilding the Temple and bringing in an age of universal peace.

A **covenant** is a promise or agreement between two parties. Covenants were made between God and Noah, Abraham and Moses.

Exam tip

It is important to use terms from the religions you have studied in your answers to examination questions. You will need to be able to define the concepts in each theme. The first exam question, for two marks, asks for a definition of a concept.

Beliefs and practices

REVISED

Your study of Judaism is separated into two areas:

Beliefs and teachings:
- The Nature of God
- The Messiah (Mashiach)
- Covenant
- Life on Earth
- The Afterlife

Practices:
- Worship
- The Synagogue
- Rituals
- Daily Life
- Festivals

Exam tip

Making connections

Although the chapter is divided into two sections there are many connections between the beliefs of Jews and the practices they keep. For example, because of belief in God as Creator many Jews practise the keeping of Shabbat each week. Relevant beliefs, texts and practise can be credited wherever they appear in your answers.

Differences matter

In your exam you will be expected to refer to the different attitudes and practices between Orthodox and Reform Jews. There are many different views but the chart below will help you remember why so many different views are held by people who follow the same religion.

Situation	Some situations such as avoiding idolatry and the importance of saving a life are important for all practising Jews but for other situations there will be different considerations, e.g. whether women should be rabbis.
Teachings	The central teachings referred to by Jews would be the Torah. The written Torah is the first five books of Moses: Genesis, Exodus, Leviticus, Numbers and Deuteronomy. Believed to have been given by God to Moses many Jews will consult the Torah as a source of authority. One of the main differences between Orthodox and Reform Jews is that Orthodox will observe the teachings of the written and oral Torah. Reform Jews will consider them in the light of contemporary society.
Authority	There are many other sources of authority which Jews may consult such as The Talmud and Mishnah, the teachings of historic rabbis such as Hillel and Maimonides or the rabbi from a local synagogue.
Interpretation	Many Orthodox Jews will observe the Torah literally with little or no interpretation. Many Reform Jews believe the teachings from the Torah and other sources of authority should be considered in contemporary society and not always taken literally.
Reason	As Jews believe God gave them free will so they believe it is up to them if they follow a right inclination (Yetzer ha tov) or a bad inclination (Yetzer ha ray). Studying the Torah is believed to help make a right decision.

Exam tip

There are many different beliefs, practices and teachings in Judaism. Sometimes this depends upon how observant they are; the country they originated from or the influence of their family and friends. When answering questions it is important to show this diversity, for example some Orthodox Jews might ... and, often, many Reform Jews will ... .

The nature of God

In this area of study you will be expected to know the nature of God as One, Creator, Law-giver and Judge; and the nature and significance of the *shekhinah*.

The nature of God as One, Creator, Law-giver and Judge

REVISED

The **Torah** is believed to have been given by God to Moses. Observant Jews will try to live their lives according to the teachings of the Torah.

Central to Judaism is belief in one God (monotheism). In the Torah there are many teachings about the nature of God which Jews express through their daily practice and worship.

In the table you can see the relationship between teachings from the Torah about the nature of God, beliefs and practices of many Jews today.

Key concept

The **Torah** is the first five books of Moses (Genesis, Exodus, Leviticus, Numbers and Deuteronomy. Regarded as the holiest part of the Tenakh.

Teachings	Belief	Practice
God created the world, day and night, the earth and animals. On the sixth day he created humans and gave them a special role to caretake all He has created. Genesis 1:3–5; Genesis 1:26–28	God is Creator. God alone created all life. Humans were given the responsibility to look after the environment. On the Seventh day God rested.	God as creator is celebrated at festivals, e.g. Rosh Hashanah and Shabbat. As God gave life some believe only he can take life and so are opposed to euthanasia. Importance of *pikuach nefesh* and preserving life.
Thou shalt have no other Gods before me. (Exodus 20) Hear O Israel the Lord our God, the Lord is one. (Deuteronomy 6:4, part of the Shema)	God is One. Judaism is a monotheistic religion with the worship of one God.	No statues in synagogues. Shema in the *mezuzah* and *tefillin*. Some use Ha Shem or won't write the name of God. Anything with God's name in must be buried if no longer used.
The Ten Commandments Exodus 20:1–15	God is Law-giver. He gave Moses the duties that Jews should keep. These form the framework of how a just society should live.	Orthodox Jews try to observe the duties in the Torah throughout their lives. Reform Jews amend them for the time they live in.
The Ten Commandments Exodus 20:1–15	God is Judge of how Jews follow the duties of the Torah.	At Rosh Hashanah God begins a judgement of good and bad deeds.

Now test yourself

TESTED

Making connections

Look at the sources and beliefs above and complete the following table by filling in the blanks.

Source	Belief	Practice
		Caring for the environment
		Euthanasia and abortion
		Judging criminals

Nature and significance of shekhinah

REVISED

Although God is believed to be everywhere, there are particular times and places where it is believed his presence is more strongly felt.

- Derives from 'shakan' which is used in the Torah to refer to God's dwelling on earth.
- Some Jews believe the **shekhinah** never left the Temple and that is why Israel has a special spirituality.
- Some Jews consider the shekhinah to be the feminine characteristics of God.
- It is believed that the shekhinah creates a sense of calm and peace.
- God's presence is often referred to when the Shabbat candles are lit.

Key concept

Shekhinah is the place where God's presence rests and can be felt.

Exam practice

Command terms

In the exam paper you will be asked four questions from this unit. Each of the questions will have different demands. In the chart below the meaning column has become jumbled. From the command word try to identify which would be the correct meaning.

Command	Meaning
What is meant by ... [2 marks]	Evaluation of a view from more than one perspective. These perspectives can all be 'for' the statement, all be 'against' the statement or be a mixture of both 'for' and 'against', e.g. 'Keeping the Ten Commandments is the most important part of Judaism.' Discuss this statement showing that you have considered more than one point of view. (You must refer to religion and belief in your answer.)
Describe ... [5 marks]	Definition of a key term (linked to one of the key terms identified for each unit), e.g. 'What is the meaning of shekhinah?'
Explain ... [8 marks]	Demonstrate knowledge and understanding by describing a belief, teaching, practice, event etc., e.g. Describe Jewish beliefs about resurrection.
Discuss this statement showing that you have considered more than one point of view. (You must refer to religion and belief in your answer.) [15 marks]	Demonstrate knowledge and understanding of a topic by explaining the statements made with reasoning and/or evidence, e.g.: ● Explain how ... ● Explain why ... ● Explain the main features of ... ● Explain the importance/significance of ... e.g. 'From two different religions or two religious traditions, explain the importance of Moses to Judaism.'

Messiah (mashiach)

In this area of study you will need to know about different views about the nature and role of the **Messiah**.

It is important that you remember you need to know about the Jewish beliefs about the Messiah. These are very different to Christian beliefs.

In Judaism it is more important to consider this life than to consider life and events to come. As there are no direct teachings about the Messiah in the Torah there are many different interpretations and beliefs. Generally, it is believed a Messianic Age will be one of peace on earth.

Key concept

The **Messiah** is the anointed one who some Jews believe will bring in a new era or age for humankind. This will include rebuilding the Temple and bringing in an age of universal peace.

Different views of the Messiah within Judaism

REVISED

- Many Jews pray for a messianic age which they believe will be one of peace on earth, bring Jews back to Israel and restore the Temple in Jerusalem.
- Messiah comes from the Hebrew Mashiach, meaning anointed. This refers to the placing of oil on the head of a king showing they are trusted by God.
- Maimonides in the twelfth century said a belief in the Messiah is central to Judaism. The traditional view is that he will be a great political leader who will bring the world to an end.
- Many Reform Jews believe it is important to focus on the good actions of humans that bring about an age of peace.
- Some Orthodox Jews believe that God has a date for the coming of the Messiah. Others believe the Messiah will come when most needed.

Exam tip

In the exam you will be asked to describe and explain. These are two different skills. When describing it is important to consider what are the main details you are going to write about. When explaining, then you must be able to think about why.

Now test yourself

TESTED

From the information above answer each of the following:

1 What will the Messiah do?
2 Who will be the Messiah?
3 When will the Messiah come?

Covenant

In this area of study you will need to know about the meaning and significance of the **covenants** made with Abraham and Moses and the importance of the Ten Commandments.

In Judaism the relationship with God is seen as a covenant; it is like a contract when promises are made between two parties.

Key concept

A **covenant** is a promise or agreement between two parties. Covenants were made between God and Noah, Abraham and Moses.

The meaning and significance of God's covenant with Abraham

REVISED

In the book of Genesis the three main parts of the covenant made between God and Abraham are described:

- God called Abraham and his family to a new land called Canaan (Genesis 12:1–3). This land is now referred to as Israel and is often called the Promised Land because of God's repeated promise to give the land to the descendants of Abraham. Jews have lived here for more than 3,200 years.
- God promised Abraham he would make a great nation from him (Genesis 17:6–8).
- God promised to bless Abraham and his family. As a part of the covenant God gave Abraham the rite of circumcision (Genesis 17:11–14). Jewish male children are usually circumcised the eighth day after birth to reflect their relationship with God.

The meaning and significance of God's covenant with Moses

REVISED

- Moses had a special relationship with God and is considered the greatest prophet.
- Moses was chosen by God to lead the Israelites out of slavery in Egypt, but Moses thought he was not capable. God, however, promised to be with him (Exodus 3:11–15).
- Moses is believed to be the only person who has seen God face to face.
- Moses was given the Torah by God on Mount Sinai. Orthodox Jews believe he was also given the oral Torah, the commentary which discusses the written Torah.
- Moses established a covenant with God. As God's chosen people the Israelites would keep the Commandments.

Now test yourself

TESTED

Look at the bullet points above for Abraham and Moses and decide if each bullet point relates to the meaning, the significance or importance, or both.

Exam tip

It is important that you know what your exam specification requires you to know and be able to explain. As the specification asks you to know the meaning and significance of the covenants with Abraham and Moses, then questions can be asked on the meaning, the significance or both.

Importance of the Ten Commandments

REVISED

- The Ten Commandments were given by God to Moses.
- They should be followed by all Jews.
- They are the duties required of humans for their creator God.
- They are the duties required for relationships between humans.
- They form the beliefs and practices of Judaism.

The Ten Commandments (Exodus 20:2–14) are an important part of your study. You will not be asked to write them all out but you should know what each of them says and how they relate to other parts of your study.

The importance of the Ten Commandments can be seen in other areas of Judaism. The table below shows some of these connections.

Exam tip

Use of sacred texts

If you can refer to relevant sources of wisdom, or sacred texts to support your answer it will help you get high marks. You don't need to remember the exact words or references, but state in your own words what they say and how believers interpret them.

Making connections

Commandments	Connections
I am God Your Lord who has brought you out of Egypt from the place of slavery.	Celebration of Passover
Do not have any other gods before me.	Importance of the Shema Prayer No statues in synagogues
Remember the Sabbath to keep it holy.	Preparing and celebrating Shabbat
Do not commit adultery.	Jewish attitudes towards marriage and relationships
Do not commit murder.	Importance of *pikuach nefesh* (saving of life)

Exam tip

In your answers you can gain marks by making connections and applying relevant knowledge and text references from different areas of study. That means that what you have learnt in Judaism can be applied to questions in philosophy and ethics. The Ten Commandments is an example of this.

Life on earth

In this area of study you will be expected to know the beliefs and teachings about *pikuach nefesh* (saving of life) and the relationship between free will and the 613 *mitzvot* (duties) between humans and with God.

The nature and importance of *pikuach nefesh*

REVISED

What is *pikuach nefesh*?	The saving of a life. This might include breaking a mitzvah, e.g. working on Shabbat or eating non-kosher food.
Why is *pikuach nefesh* important?	God created life (Psalm 139:13–15) in his image (Genesis 1:26–27) . Therefore, life is seen as sacred. Therefore, life is sacred. To save a life (*pikuach nefesh*) takes priority over all but three of the *mitzvot* (idolatry, incest and adultery).
What impact does *pikuach nefesh* have today?	Many Jews will consider *pikuach nefesh* when making decisions about life and death issues. However, they should be able to prove that a life will be actually be saved. Some Jews consider the teachings of Jeremiah 1:5 or teachings from the Talmud (Yoma 84b) when making decisions about when life begins.

Now test yourself

TESTED

Select two of the following and explain how *pikuach nefesh* might be relevant.

- Should the death penalty be reintroduced?
- Should abortion be legal?
- Should euthanasia be legal?
- Should contraception be allowed?
- Should everyone have to carry a transplant donor card?
- Should an Orthodox Jewish doctor work on Shabbat?

Relationship between 613 *mitzvot* and free will

REVISED

Jews will keep the ***mitzvot*** in different ways. They believe God gave them free will to choose to follow the *mitzvot* or not. Some of the 613 *mitzvot* are no longer relevant as they relate to the Temple, which was destroyed.

613 *Mitzvot*
In the Torah there are 613 duties. Orthodox Jews try to observe as many of the 613 as they can. Reform Jews say that some are not relevant to twenty-first century.

Both
Some Jews see the *mitzvot* as a guide-line, others as a path to follow or be punished. All believe people have free will.

Free will
The Torah teaches God has given Jews freedom to chose what is right or wrong. Each Jew is believed to be born with two inclinations – to do good or bad. Studying the Torah can help humans choose to do good.

Key concept

Mitzvot is a term that has a mix of meanings: it is most often used to refer to duties (such as the 613 in the Torah) and good deeds.

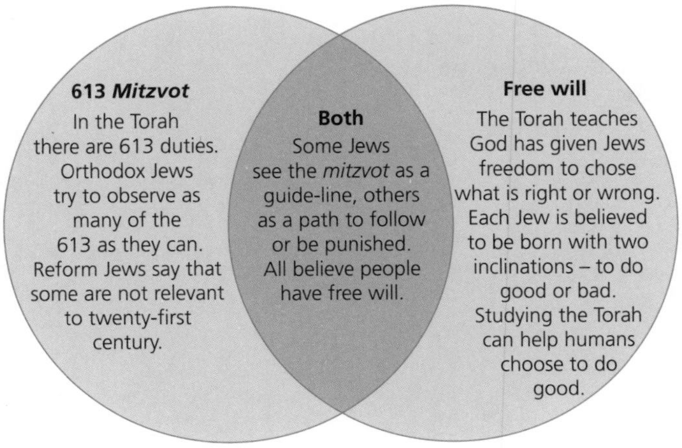

Making connections

In component 1, Foundational Catholic Theology, you are required to study the themes where appropriate from the Jewish tradition. The table below gives some areas where you can make connections between Jewish teachings, beliefs and the component 1 content.

Teachings	Belief	Link to component 1
God created humans in his image. (Genesis 1:26–27)	All human life is sacred as created by God in his image.	Beliefs about the origin and sanctity of life (Theme 1: Origins and meaning)
People should live not die by the Torah (Talmud B Yoma 84b)	Preserving life is more important than observing the Torah.	Issues related to sanctity of life, e.g. abortion (Theme 1: Origins and meaning)
When I had not yet formed you in the womb,I knew you. (Jeremiah 1:5)	God's relationship with humans begins before they are born.	Issues related to sanctity of life, e.g. abortion (Theme 1: Origins and meaning)
That which is hateful to you do not do to your neighbour. That is the whole of the Torah. (Hillel)	The most important duty of the Torah is to treat others as you would want to be treated.	Dignity of human beings (Theme 1: Origins and meaning)
From his dwelling places he watches all who live on earth. (Psalm 33:14)	God has given free will but watches those who do good and evil acts.	Good, evil and suffering (Theme 2: Good and evil)

Exam practice

Below are a number of points that could be included in an answer to:

Keeping the Ten Commandments is the most important part of Judaism. [15 marks]

Discuss this statement showing that you have considered more than one point of view. (You must refer to religion and belief in your answer.)

Select four points from the numbered statements below that you think are most important and use them to form your evaluation to the question. In your response, you must make sure you:

- select alternative or different viewpoints
- show how belief influences individuals, communities and societies
- form judgements
- take no longer than 15 minutes to write your response.

1 The Ten Commandments are important as given by God.
2 There are many other *mitzvot* that are important.
3 Different traditions in Judaism keep Shabbat in different ways.
4 *Pikuach nefesh* is more important than Shabbat regulations.
5 Importance of belief in one God as in the shema.
6 Importance of the Ten Commandments are shown in the synagogue.

Exam tip

D-type evaluation questions

There are two evaluation questions in each exam paper. These are very important as each one is worth 15 marks. Look at the demands of the d-type question here. To achieve high marks your response needs much more than the explanation of a number of points.

The afterlife

In this area of study you will need to know about the beliefs and teachings about life after death, judgement and resurrection.

- Jews focus on life not afterlife as the ways of God are unknown:
- The afterlife is called 'olam ha-ba' – the world to come.
- It is important to live life in preparation for the world to come.
- The Mishnah states 'This world is like a lobby before the olam ha ba. Prepare yourself in the lobby.'
- There are many different beliefs between and within Orthodox and Reform Jews about life after death. These arise from different interpretations of texts in the Torah.

Jewish beliefs about life after death

REVISED

What will olam ha ba be like?	Sometimes known as the 'immortality of the soul'. Many Orthodox Jews believe in some form of resurrection – physically or spiritually. Many Reform Jews don't believe in resurrection but that the soul lives on.
When will it happen?	Some Jews believe the resurrection of the dead will come during the Messianic Age. Some argue it will happen after the Messianic Age.
Who will be raised?	Some argue only the righteous will be resurrected; others that everyone will be resurrected but then a day of Judgement will come.

Now test yourself

TESTED

Throughout this study of Jewish beliefs and teachings differences between Orthodox and Reform traditions have been identified.

In the Venn diagram, which of these do you think most Orthodox and Reform Jews would believe in and which would both believe in?

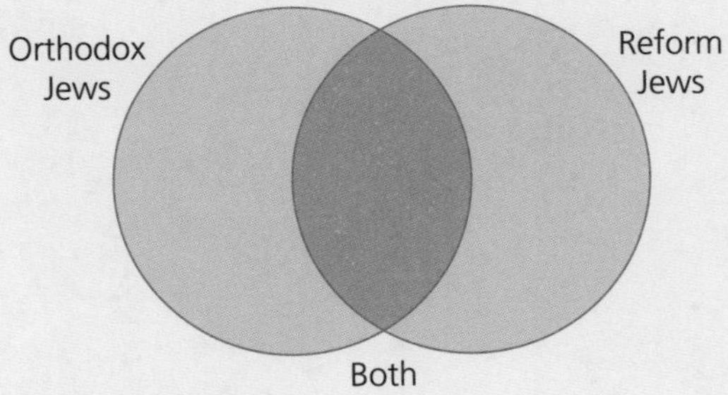

- Belief in one God.
- The importance of *pikuach nefesh* – saving a life.
- Importance in observing all the *mitzvot* (duties).
- After death, everyone will be resurrected.
- It's what you do on earth that is more important than thinking about what will happen.
- Moses is a special person.
- God created the world in seven days.

Exam practice

In the exam the second question of each unit will usually be a b-type question. This question is worth five marks. One of the skills in answering the question is selecting the main points that answer the question.

The question has been asked:

b Describe different Jewish beliefs about resurrection. [5 marks]

The answer given was:

There are many different Jewish views about what happens in the afterlife in Judaism. Some say Jews are raised from the dead when they die but others believe when you die that's it. There are different views about when Jews might be raised from the dead.

Look at the marking grids on page vii. How many marks would you give this answer?

The mark given for this was:

Level 1 – 1 Mark: A limited statement of information about the religious idea, belief, practice, teaching or concept. A limited understanding of how belief influences individuals, communities and societies.

Consider:

- Were specific details given in this answer?
- Where in the answer are religious/specialist language and terms and/or sources of wisdom and authority used?

Compare with this answer which was given 5 marks.

Many Orthodox Jews believe in resurrection. Some consider only the soul will be raised not the body. Members of Reform Judaism often reject resurrection and often believing that the soul lives on after death rather than a resurrection. Some Jews believe that on Judgment Day, Jews will be raised from the dead, beginning with those buried on Mount Zion in Jerusalem.

Worship: practices in Britain and elsewhere

In this area of study you will need to know about the nature and importance of **synagogue** services; the different ways that worship happens in the home and items that may be worn for worship.

The nature and importance of synagogue services

REVISED

The synagogue is more than a place of worship for Jews. It is a place for study and often a centre for the community. There are differences between Orthodox and Reform synagogues, not just in design but also in ways of worship.

Key concept

A **synagogue** is the house of assembly; building for Jewish public prayer, study and assembly.

For your exam you will need to know three important examples of worship:

- Shabbat services
- prayer
- the Amidah.

Shabbat services

When do Shabbat services happen?	Usually services are held on Shabbat eve (the Friday night), and late Shabbat afternoon (Saturday afternoon).
What happens at a Shabbat service?	The Shabbat morning service includes important prayers (e.g. Shema and Amidah), the *haftorah* is read, rabbis deliver a weekly sermon. After the service a Kiddush is held. In the Reform Synagogue less Hebrew is used and instruments may be played.
Why are Shabbat services important?	They bring the Jewish community together. They are able to listen to the rabbi's sermon which is based on the readings of the week. They are able to take part in communal prayers.

Prayer

REVISED

- Through prayer Jews believe they can communicate with God, forming a bridge between humans and God.
- Prayers can be said individually or collectively, such as at Shabbat.
- Prayer is a part of daily life. Observant Jews will pray before performing *mitzvot*, going to bed at night and seeing unusual things such as rainbows.
- There are three different types of prayer: praising God, requests of God and thanksgiving.
- Some Jews believe it's important to understand the prayer and so will recite them in English; other Jews believe it's important to use Hebrew as it connects Jews worldwide and is considered a holy language.

The Amidah

What is the Amidah?	The Amidah is a prayer at the core of every Jewish worship service and is so important it is often called 'the prayer'.
What happens during the Amidah?	Amidah means 'standing' and people stand throughout the prayer. It has 18 blessings which forms three types of prayer: praise of God, requests of God and thanksgiving. It is recited silently and then repeated by the rabbi or cantor.
Why is it important?	The Amidah signifies being in God's presence. It is said standing to show this and at the end three steps are taking backwards, bowing to both sides, and three steps taken forwards to formally show retreating from God's symbolic presence. It contains three types of prayer to communicate with God: praise, requests and thanksgiving.

Now test yourself

TESTED

Acrostics are words where the initial letter triggers the beginning of another word. They can be useful in remembering key facts about something. From this section on the synagogue select important features and functions beginning with each of the letters for synagogue and explain the connection.

Worship in the home

REVISED

If you are looking for God, go home

Preparing and celebrating for festivals

- Many festivals such as Pesach are prepared for and celebrated in the home.
- Each week Shabbat is remembered and celebrated in the home reflecting the Commandment to remember and keep the seventh day as in the Ten Commandments (Exodus 20).

Recitation of prayers

- Prayers in the home are said.
- Orthodox Jews on waking will often say the Modeh Ani to thank God when they wake up.
- Many families will have a *siddur* (prayer book) which they use at home.

Display of Mezuzah

- A *mezuzah* case is often on the doors (apart from the bathroom). Inside the case is a *mezuzah*: a scroll containing the Shema – the central prayer of Judaism.
- For many, the Mezuzah symbolises God's protection of the house and that the family should live according to the Shema.

Keeping kosher

Obeying Jewish laws regarding what are fit and proper things to eat and actions to take.

Jewish values

- The home is where children learn about what is important in life.
- The value of justice is often shown through charity collections in a *pushke* box.

Preparation and celebration of Shabbat

REVISED

Although celebrated weekly, **Shabbat** is important for worship in both the home and synagogue. There are many differences to how Orthodox and Reform Jews might celebrate Shabbat but it is generally considered a time to focus on the important things of life.

What ways do Jews prepare for Shabbat?	Each family celebrates Shabbat in their own way. For many Orthodox Jews they will not work during Shabbat. This means that the preparation for the Saturday meals must be done before. Special foods, e.g. the *challot* loaves, need to have been bought and the Shabbat table laid. Most important all the family need to be home before the candles are lit to bring the presence of Shabbat in the home.
What happens during Shabbat?	For many Orthodox Jews no work will be done unless it involves saving life. This means that driving and cooking is not allowed nor the carrying of anything. The woman of the family lights two candles to bring the presence of Shabbat into the home. There will be a blessing over the *challot* (loaves) and a Kiddush prayer recited over a cup of wine. On the Saturday morning most families will go to synagogue. At sunset on Saturday a *havdallah* candle is lit to symbolise the distinction between Shabbat and the rest of the week. A glass of wine is passed around and a spice box is sniffed to symbolise the hope of a sweet week.
Why is Shabbat important?	Keeping Shabbat obeys the *mitzvah* 'to remember' and to 'keep it holy' (Exodus 20:8). It is remembered as a celebration of God's creation. It is 'kept' through worship in the home and the synagogue. It is often seen as a gift from God when weekday worries can be forgotten and families can be together. As the woman of the family lights the candles so it is believed the presence of Shabbat bringing peace is brought into the home.

Key concept

Shabbat is the day of spiritual renewal and rest. Beginning at sunset on Friday and closing at nightfall Saturday.

Exam tip

There are many different ways that Jews worship in the home. Differences occur not only between Orthodox and Reform traditions but within Orthodox and Reform families.

Exam practice

In the following question the three main areas of the explanation have been identified but each point needs expanding. You have eight minutes to do this. Make sure you have used a range of relevant religious language in each of your answers.

Explain why Shabbat is important. [8 marks]

- It remembers God's creation, as in Genesis it states ...
- It is a time for spiritual renewal and meeting with the family and Jewish community. This is shown through ...
- It is one of the Ten Commandments which ...

Exam tip

C-type questions will ask for an explanation. This could be how? Why? Where? What? etc. It helps to underline whether you are being asked to explain how, why, what, and so on, as the focus of your answer would be different.

As 8 marks are awarded for this question you should be giving at least three developed explanations which use religious language.

Items worn for worship

REVISED

Tefillin

What is *tefillin*?	Made up of two leather boxes, each containing part of the Shema prayer. The *tefillah shel rosh* is bound to the head with straps and the *tefillah shel yad* is bound to the upper arm with straps.
Who wears it?	Usually worn by Orthodox males after their bar mitzvah on weekday mornings during prayers but not on Shabbat or at festivals. Some women, especially from Reform Judaism wear *tefillin*.
Why is it worn?	It obeys the *mitzvah* in the Torah (Deuteronomy 6:8). A prayer is said when the *tefillin* is in place: 'Blessed are You, Lord our God, King of the Universe, who has sanctified us with his commandments as to wear *tefillin*.' They are a reminder that the wearer must serve God through developing good thoughts and through acts of compassion.

Tallith

What is *tallith*?	A four-cornered garments with fringes (*tzizit*). There are two types: *tallit gadol* (large), a large garment of wool or silk worn across the back, which is often called a prayer shawl. The *tallit katan* (small) is worn under everyday clothes with the *tzizit* hanging down at the corners.
When is it worn?	Many Orthodox and some Reform Jews will wear the *tallit gadol* during prayers and worship. The *tallit katan* is worn by some Orthodox Jews throughout the day.
Why is it worn?	Wearing the *tzizit* relates to the duty to wear fringes in the corner of clothes (Number 15).

Kippah

What is *kippah*?	A head covering which can be of different designs and colours.
When is it worn?	It can be worn from childhood. Some Jews choose to wear it during prayer and when in synagogue but others wear it all the time when awake. Many male Orthodox and Reform Jews wear the *kippah* but there are also some Reform Jewish women who wear it.
Why is it worn?	The exact meaning is unknown although it is often seen as a sign of respect for God as the highest part of the head is covered. It is also seen as a symbol of Jewish identity.

The synagogue

In this area of study you will need to know about the main features of a synagogue and the importance of the *bimah*, *aron hakodesh*, Torah scrolls, *ner tamid*, seating and *minyan*.

You will be expected to be able to describe and explain how Orthodox and Reform synagogues are places for worship, social and community activities.

Features of a synagogue: *bimah*

REVISED

Synagogues will have many different designs depending upon their observances and locality. None, however, will have any statues or representation of living beings as commanded by God in Exodus 20:4–5.

What is a *bimah*?	A raised platform from which the Torah scrolls are read.
What are the differences?	In Orthodox synagogues it is usually in the middle so the rabbi faces the congregation. In Reform Judaism the *bimah* is at the front combined with the ark.
Why is it important?	It has central focus for the reading of the Torah scrolls and the sermons preached. This shows that the Torah should be central to life.

Features of a synagogue: *aron hakodesh*

REVISED

What is the *aron hakodesh*?	Also known as the ark this is where the Torah scrolls are kept. During some prayers the doors and curtain of the ark may be opened or closed.
What are the differences?	In Sephardic synagogues it is called the *heikhal*, and the curtain is usually inside the doors of the ark.
Why is it important?	It is the most important place of the synagogue as it contains the Torah scrolls. Its importance is shown by its placement in the wall facing Jerusalem. The opening and closing of the ark signifies important times, e.g. it is open for the ten days of penitence between Rosh Hashanah and Yom Kippur. Its importance is shown by the *ner tamid* above it and when the ark doors are open the congregation usually stands.

Features of a synagogue: Torah scrolls

REVISED

What are the Torah scrolls?	These are the scrolls that contain the Torah. They are made from animal skins and handwritten by a trained scribe. The scroll is attached to two staves known as the tree of life. Each scroll is wrapped when not used and decorated with silver. The scrolls are carried to the *bimah* to be read.
What are the differences?	In some Sephardic synagogues, the scroll is kept in a metal or wooden case.
Why are they important?	A portion of the Torah scroll is used in each Shabbat service. To show its importance it will be raised to show the congregation. It is seen as an honour or *mitzvah* to be called up to read from the Torah.

Features of a synagogue: *ner tamid*

REVISED

What is the *ner tamid*?	Often called the eternal lamp the *ner tamid* is placed above the *aron hakodesh* or ark. It always burns and should never be put out.
What are the differences between Orthodox and Reform Synagogues?	There may be differences in design depending upon the country of the synagogue and whether it is Sephardic or Ashkenazi.
Why is it important?	A symbol of God's presence. In Exodus 27:20–21, Jews were told 'to cause a lamp to burn continually'. It is a symbol of the golden menorah which burned constantly in the Temple. The *ner tamid* is also considered to stand for the light of the Torah, which it is placed over.

Features of a synagogue: seating arrangements

REVISED

What are the seating arrangements in a synagogue?	The seating arrangements reflect the type of synagogue.
What are the differences?	In Orthodox synagogues there will be separate seating for men and women with women often sitting in a gallery. In Reform synagogues everyone sits together. Ashkenazi synagogues have all the worshippers facing the same direction while Sephardi synagogues have the seats all around the walls.
Why are they important?	The seating is one of the main differences between Orthodox and Reform synagogues.

Features of a synagogue: *minyan*

REVISED

What is the *minyan*?	Some prayers require a community of worshippers which is defined as ten people.
What are the differences?	Many Reform synagogues no longer have *minyans* or allow a mixed *minyan* of men and women. Most Orthodox synagogues only allow men after their bar mitzvah to form the *minyan*.
Why is it important?	The Amidah, Priestly Benediction and Kaddish cannot be recited without a *minyan*.

Worship, social and community functions of a synagogue

REVISED

- Synagogues are houses of prayer where Jews can pray together.
- Some prayers can only be said where there is a *minyan* (ten people) so many observant Jews will go to a synagogue each day.
- Synagogues are houses of study with libraries of texts.
- Children will go to a synagogue to learn about their religion.
- Synagogues arrange a programme of social events. These might include support for the elderly and ill, sports activities and charity collections.

There are many similarities between synagogues such as:

- Facing Jerusalem where the Temple stood
- No statues to obey Exodus 20:8–10
- In the Midrash it states: God asks, 'Is there anyone who came to the synagogue and did not find My presence there?'

Exam practice

In your d-type questions, you need to select different points and state if they are a strong argument or not.

John has been asked if synagogues are important today in Britain. He has thought of a number of points but hasn't given any further explanation or details. Select four from the list below and explain why they are most important.

- People can pray anywhere.
- There are a decreasing number of Jews to worship at the synagogue.
- Some prayers require a *minyan*.
- Synagogues organise social and community activities.
- Synagogues are often too big and expensive for the number of worshippers.
- There can be difficulties in getting a rabbi.
- Synagogues are houses of study.

Exam tip

It is important to know what each of the features of a synagogue are and also to be able to explain why they are important. Remember that there may be differences between Orthodox and Reform practice and also Asheknazi and Sephardic tradition.

Now test yourself

TESTED

Copy the Venn diagram to sort out which of these statements you think Orthodox or Reform Jews would say.

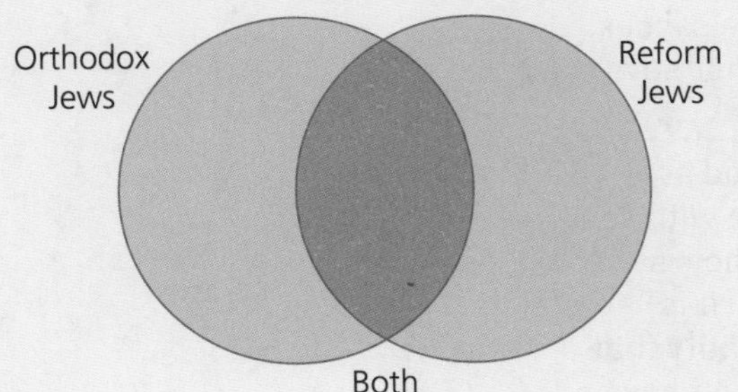

- We have a woman rabbi.
- Shabbat is brought into the home by a woman.
- Women and men should sit separately in a synagogue.
- A *tallith* is worn when I worship.
- Observing the oral and written Torah guides my actions and decisions.
- Men and women can read from the Torah scrolls.
- The Amidah is an important prayer.
- At the synagogue we have a community hall.

Rituals

Rituals (ceremonies consisting of a series of actions) play an important role in Judaism.

Relationship with God is established through each ritual. Sometimes this will be through a particular action, for example, circumcision or through performing a *mitzvah* stated in the Torah.
Identity of being Jewish is reinforced through the ritual in front of the Jewish community.
Traditions of Judaism are kept. The rituals have been a historically important part of Judaism. For example, it was through a covenant between God and Abraham that the ritual of brit milah began.
Unity amongst Jews is shown through the ritual. At burial everyone should be treated the same to show there is no difference between rich and poor. Often the Jewish community will support in the preparation of a ritual such as the burial society.
Affirms faith in God from the individual as each ritual often includes prayers.
Lifecycle of a Jew involves rituals from birth to death. This shows the continual relationship between a Jew and God throughout life.

Role and importance of brit milah

REVISED

Who has a brit milah?	Eight-day-old boy babies or males converting to Judaism.
What happens during the ceremony?	A *mohel* will circumcise the baby on the eighth day after birth. Usually only men attend the ceremony although there will be women as well in Reform ceremonies. The baby is placed on an empty chair (Elijah's chair). Then the baby is placed on the lap of the *sandek*. After the circumcision the father says a blessing.
Why is brit milah important?	It shows a relationship with God as it represents the covenant made with Abraham. During the brit the boy is given his Hebrew name. The brit is such an important form of identity that men converting to Judaism must have a circumcision in Orthodox Judaism.

Bar mitzvah

REVISED

Who has a bar mitzvah?	Usually Jewish boys have a bar mitzvah ceremony on the Shabbat after their 13th birthday.
What happens in a bar mitzvah?	Before a bar mitzvah the boy is taught about the importance of prayer and learns Hebrew so he can read his portion from the Torah in the synagogue. The boy is called up to the *bimah* in the synagogue to recite a blessing and read his part of the Torah. Friends and relatives watch. His father then recites a statement in which he thanks God. This is usually followed by a form of celebration.
Why is a bar mitzvah important?	It is a sign of entering into manhood and building a relationship with God. After a bar mitzvah boys can form part of the *minyan* (group of ten people needed for some prayers). They are believed to be responsible enough to keep the *mitzvot* in the Torah. Some Jewish boys will start to wear *tefillin* for prayers.

Bat mitzvah and bat chayil

REVISED

Who has a bat mitzvah/bat chayil?	A celebration for girls. Usually girls do not have large ceremonies and some have no ceremonies at all. Some Orthodox girls have a bat chayil ceremony (daughter of worth) instead. Some Reform have a bat mitzvah. Often both ceremonies happen at the age of 12.
What happens in a bat mitzvah/bat Chayil?	There are many different types of celebrations which often depend upon the traditions of the family. Usually bat mitzvahs will include a special service in the synagogue and a presentation of her learning. Reform Jews might read from the Torah scrolls during the service.
Why is bat mitzvah/bat chayil important?	Usually girls do not have such large ceremonies as a bar mitzvah as they are not required to do the same duties as boys. In Reform Judaism after the bat mitzvah girls may be part of the *minyan* and read from the Torah scrolls.

Marriage

REVISED

Who has a marriage ceremony?	In Reform Judaism same-sex marriages are allowed as well as male and female weddings. Orthodox Judaism does not recognise same-sex marriages.
What happens in a marriage ceremony?	Ceremonies can happen in synagogues, hotels or open spaces. There should be a *chuppah* under which the rabbi conducts the ceremony. The *kiddushin* (holy) is the first part of the ceremony. It is often called the betrothal ceremony. The second part of the ceremony is the *nisuin* in which seven further blessings are said to finalise the marriage. Rings are exchanged. The bride normally wears a ring on her index finger. The marriage contract or *ketubah* is signed by bride and groom. This is an important legal document. At the end of the ceremony a glass is stamped on by the groom.
Why are marriage ceremonies important?	It fulfils the duty in the Torah to: 'A man shall therefore leave his father and mother and be united with his wife, and they shall become one flesh' (Genesis 2.24). So it allows for the bearing of children and to 'be fruitful and multiply'. By taking place under the *chuppah* symbolises the importance of the Jewish home.

Mourning rituals

REVISED

Who is involved in mourning rituals?	There are many differences which often depend upon the individual families. The *onan* is the main mourner who will take charge of the funeral. The *chevra kadisha* is the burial society attached to the synagogue and they will prepare the body.
What are the mourning rituals?	The funeral is simple with psalms often read. Once the grave is filled then the *kaddish* is recited. The *kaddish* is a prayer declaring God's greatness. After the funeral for seven days mourners will sit *shiva*, usually by staying in their home. During this time they will be visited by members of the synagogue and male mourners will recite the *kaddish*. There will usually be no music played in the house and a candle kept burning. A *yahrzeit* ceremony is held each year to mark the death. Prayers are said and a candle burns for 24 hours.
Why are mourning rituals important?	The body is believed to be the earthly container for the soul so it is important that it is treated with great respect before it is buried. The mourning pattern after the funeral shows that life can't go on as before.

In this area of study there are a lot of terms you need to know. It is important that you know these terms and can use them in your answers.

Now test yourself

TESTED

Look at the words below and match them with the correct definition.

Word	Definition
Brit milah	Ritual that can happen when a girl is 12. Means daughter of the commandment.
Bar mitzvah	Ritual that happens when a boy 13. Means son of the commandment. From now on he can join a *minyan*.
Bat mitzvah	Circumcision of eight-day-old boy babies which is a symbol of the covenant with Abraham.
Onan	The anniversary of a death.
Kaddish	Wedding canopy.
Sheva	Prayer publicly said by mourners.
Yarzheit	Main mourner.
Chevra kaddisha	Burial society associated with a synagogue.
Chuppah	Person trained to do the brit milah.
Mohel	Seven days of intense mourning following a death. During this time no work is done.

Daily life

In this area of study you will consider how Judaism is practised through daily life. You will need to know how the Tenakh and the Talmud are used and the requirements, benefits and challenges of keeping a kosher diet.

Significance of use of the Tenakh and the Talmud

REVISED

Torah is the five books of Moses (Genesis, Exodus, Leviticus, Numbers and Deuteronomy). It is the holiest part of the Tenakh. Jews will try to follow the *mitzvot* of the Torah in their daily life. Passages from the Torah are read each week in the synagogue and in rituals such as bar mitzvah.

Tenakh is made up of the Torah, the Neviim (Prophets) and the Ketuvim (writings).

The Neviim (prophets) are books of the prophets which are studied to learn about the history of Judaism. Extracts are read each week in the Shabbat service.

The Ketuvim (writings) records how Jews behaved towards God. It includes the Psalms which are often recited in worship.

The Mishnah contains the Oral Torah, the Halakah (teachings on issues of Law) and the Haggadah (guidance on teaching).

The Talmud is a combination of the Mishnah and the Gemara. When extracts from the Torah are unclear then the Talmud often gives further explanation.

The Gemara is the commentary on the Mishnah which gives further details and guidance on issues of law and worship.

Dietary law

REVISED

In Leviticus Chapter 11, there are details regarding the foods that can and cannot be eaten in Judaism. There are many differences amongst Jews as to how far they keep the **kosher** diet.

Kosher laws date back to the Torah where there are many references about what can and can't be eaten, e.g. Leviticus 11:1–23. Keeping a kosher diet also includes the way in which the food is prepared.

Observant Jews will often refuse to eat the meat of certain animals, e.g. pork, shellfish, and ensuring that meat dishes aren't mixed with milk foods.

Shechitah is the method used to prepare kosher meat. This includes what is supposed to be a less painful way of killing the animal. This is done by a Jew called a *shochet* who kills the animal as a form of dedication to God. The Torah commands Jews not to eat the blood of animals and birds so the blood is drained away.

Homes in which families keep kosher will often have two sets of pans and fridges. One will be for meat produces and one for milk products as meat and milk products shouldn't be eaten in the same meal.

Eating meat and milk products in one meal is forbidden by observant Jews. This means that meals will be of meat products without any butter, milk or cheese, or milk products without any meat. Some foods such as vegetables and eggs are called *parev* and can be eaten with either meat meals or milk meals.

Reform Jews will adapt the kosher regulations for their own lifestyle. Some will eat meat and milk products together but refuse to eat shellfish or pork products.

Key concept

Kosher means 'fit' or 'proper'. Foods that are permitted to be eaten according to Leviticus 11 are kosher. It is also used to refer to the purity of ritual objects such as Torah scrolls.

On the one hand:

- Keeping the *mitzvot* that is in the Torah.
- Part of Jewish tradition that has been passed down through history.
- Part of Jewish identity binding together the Jewish community.

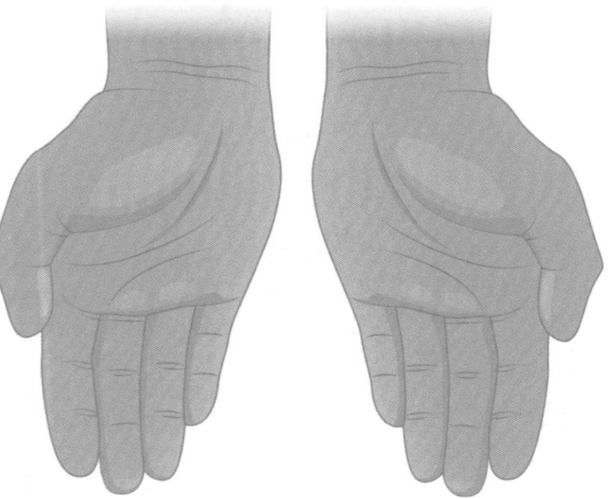

On the other hand:

- There are few kosher shops in Britain.
- Kosher food is often very expensive.
- It is difficult to eat out socially and keep a kosher diet.

Now test yourself

TESTED

Create a mind map to illustrate how Judaism can impact on daily life.

Festivals: practices in Britain and elsewhere

For this area of study you need to know about four different Jewish festivals. For each you need to know about the origin, meaning and celebration.

Rosh Hashanah

REVISED

Origin and meaning

- Many consider Rosh Hashanah as the day God created the world.
- Rosh means head or beginning.
- It is a happy time to celebrate the beginning of a new world.
- It is also a serious time to remember how God made the world and acts as a judge.
- Rosh Hashanah and Yom Kippur are connected in a process of judgement as many believe that on Rosh Hashanah God judges people for the deeds in the last year.

Celebration

- Special services are held in the synagogue on the eve of Rosh Hashanah.
- Special foods such as pomegranates, apples and honey will be eaten to symbolise a sweet new year ahead.
- At the morning service a *shofar* (ram's horn) is blown 100 times to represent the crying of the soul asking to be reunited with God.
- Some Jews will perform *tashlikh* when they cast away the crumbs in their pockets to symbolise their sins being cast away.
- During the next ten days Jews consider their deeds in the last year and try to apologise to anyone they have done wrong to.

Yom Kippur

REVISED

Origin and meaning

- Often called Day of Atonement.
- Holiest day of the year.
- It is the end of the ten days of repentance.
- A day of self-denial with a fast throughout the day.
- Many people will spend the day in the synagogue.

Celebration

- Often food and money is given to help the poor.
- Some more observant Jews will visit the *mikveh* (pool of natural water) for a spiritual cleaning before Yom Kippur.
- During Yom Kippur, many Jews will fast for 25 hours.
- In the synagogue, the Kol Nidrei (All Vows) is sung and the story of Jonah is told. During the prayers Jews will confess their sins to God. The service ends with the reciting of the Shema.
- After nightfall, a single blast of the *shofar* marks the end of the service.

Pesach

REVISED

Origin and meaning

- Pesach celebrates the freedom from slavery in Egypt which was led by Moses.
- It is often called Passover as God passed over the houses of the Israelites during the final plague.
- In the book of Exodus, God commanded that the festival should be held each year (Exodus 12.14).
- Many of the foods eaten during the festival have special meaning. Foods without leaven (grain products that can swell) are eaten such as *matzah* as a remembrance that the Israelites left Egypt before the bread had time to rise.
- The festival is often called the Festival of Freedom and prayers are said each year for people not free.

Celebration

- Before Pesach begins the house needs to be rid of all its *chametz* (foods which have grain products that can swell).
- Families often attend synagogue and then go home for a special *seder* meal.
- At the *seder* meal the table will contain a *seder* dish on which there will be symbolic foods (lambs bone, roasted egg, a green vegetable to dip in salt water, bitter herbs and a paste made of apples, walnut and wine).
- At the *seder* meal prayers will be read from a special book called the Haggadah.
- The door will be left open and a glass of wine left for the Prophet Elijah who some Jews believe will return at the end of Pesach to announce the coming of the Messiah.

Sukkot

REVISED

Origin and meaning

- An important harvest festival that is counted as a *mitzvah*.
- Remembers the 40-year period when the Israelites were in the desert on their way to the Promised Land.
- Shelters or booths (*sukkahs*) are made which represents the temporary shelter that were used in the desert. Families will often eat and some sleep in the *sukkah*.
- Two special objects are used during the festival. An *etrog* (citrus fruit) and a *lulav* (palm, myrtle and willow placed in a wooden holder).
- Bringing the four species together is a reminder that Jews should be united.

Celebration

- Sukkot lasts for seven days and many Jews do not work on the first and second day.
- Jewish families build a *sukkah* (temporary booth) with a roof that the stars can be seen through. Families will often eat and some sleep in the *sukkah*.
- *Sukkahs* are often decorated with prayers and pictures of fruit and harvests.
- On each morning (apart from Shabbat) the *lulav* is waved and a blessing is said to God.
- Many synagogues have a *sukkah*.

Now test yourself

TESTED

Sort the words into the table under the festival they are associated with.

- Moses
- Egypt
- *sukkah*
- desert
- *Seder*
- seven days
- *mitzvah*
- creation
- New Year
- Day of Atonement
- *Kol Nidrei*
- *Lulav*
- harvest festival
- *Chametz*
- Prophet Elijah
- pomegranates
- tashlich
- *fasting*
- Shema
- *Kol Nidrei*

Rosh Hashanah	Yom Kippur	Sukkot	Pesach

Knowledge check

Question a) is always about definitions of key concepts. Make sure you know them.

Use the look, cover, write and check technique to learn them. Look at the concept. Cover it and then write it down. Finally check your answer.

Synagogue	House of assembly; building for Jewish public prayer, study and assembly.
Shekinhah	The place where God's presence rests and can be felt.
Shabbat	Day of spiritual renewal and rest. Beginning at sunset on Friday and closing at nightfall on Saturday.
Kosher	('fit' or 'proper') Foods that are permitted to be eaten according to Leviticus Chapter 11. It is also used to refer to the purity of ritual objects such as Torah scrolls.
Torah	The five books of Moses (Genesis, Exodus, Leviticus, Numbers and Deuteronomy). Regarded as the holiest books of the Tenakh.
Mitzvot	The term has a mix of meanings. It is often used to refer to duties (such as the 613 in the Torah) and good deeds.
Messiah	The anointed one who Jews believe will bring in a new era or age for humankind. This will include rebuilding the Temple and bringing in an age of universal peace.
Covenant	A promise or agreement between two parties. Covenants were made between God with Noah, Abraham and Moses.

Summary questions

Beliefs

1. What is the Shema and how would a Jewish person use it?
2. What is the Torah?
3. What is the Jewish word for 'the divine presence'?
4. What does the word Messiah mean?
5. What is the main difference between Orthodox and Reform Judaism about the Messiah?
6. What is a Covenant?
7. Why is Abraham important to Jews?
8. Why is Moses the most important prophet?
9. What is Pikuach Nefesh?
10. What does *mitzvot* mean?

Practices

1. Why is Shabbat significant for Jews?
2. Give three differences between an Orthodox and Reform service.
3. What is the siddur?
4. What is a mezuzah?
5. Name three features of a synagogue.
6. Why is brit milah important for Jews?
7. What is a chuppah.
8. Describe the mourning rituals for Jews.
9. What is kosher?
10. How is Rosh Hashanah celebrated?
11. What is Pesach?

Exam focus

(a) questions

a What do Jews mean by the term 'Shekinhah'? [2]

Shekinhah means the place where God's presence is and can be felt. Jews believe God dwelt in the Temple.

This answer would get 2 marks.

(b) questions

For these questions you will be expected to describe a religious teaching, belief, idea, practice, place, event or view.

b Describe Jewish teaching on the Messiah. [5]

Activity

Using the mark scheme on page vii, write a response to this question. Remember to use religious language in your answer. See if you can use the following words:

- Messianic Age
- The Temple
- Orthodox
- Reform
- Torah
- Tenakh

Remember to include sources of authority.

(c) questions

c Explain why Moses is important in Judaism. [8]

Many Jews believe that Moses is the only person ever to have seen God and so is considered to be the greatest of all Jewish prophets. He was a great leader and led the Israelites out of slavery in Egypt and through the desert to the Promised Land. Stories about Moses as a baby, life in Egypt and time in the wilderness are in the Torah which is a sacred text for Jews. Moses was blessed with a special relationship with God as God spoke to him from of the Burning Bush and on Mount Sinai. During the time in the wilderness Moses received the Torah on Mount Sinai from God. This is the sacred text for Jews and includes the mitzvoth or duties that form a basis for Jewish life and worship.

Activity

1 Use the mark scheme on page viii to mark this answer.
2 Attempt an answer using this question, but this time for Abraham instead of Moses.

(d) questions

d 'You have to go to the synagogue to be a Jew.' Discuss the statement showing that you have considered more than one point of view. [15]

Response 1

Jewish people usually go to a synagogue for services, prayers and community events. They will try and walk there because on Saturdays they are not allowed to do any work and the synagogue might be quite far away and the walk would be tiring and feel like work. Jews like to go to the synagogue because it means you can be with people who believe what you believe and you can all join in the singing and prayers. Also, their holy books are kept there, so they would want to go and see those. I don't see the point in going to a synagogue because I am not Jewish, but I expect it is important for them.

On the other hand, you could just pray at home where you have peace and quiet to concentrate and be with family. Jewish people think that family life is important especially on a Friday and Saturday when they celebrate Sabbath.

Response 2

For many Jews attending a synagogue is an important part of their religion and a way of expressing their Jewish beliefs. Through taking part in the Shabbat services and festivals Jews become a part of a Jewish community and learn more about Judaism by listening to the sermon by the rabbi and hearing the reading from the Sefer Torah.

Some would say that a synagogue is not just used for worship as there will be a range of community events such as interfaith discussions. It is also considered a house of learning where Jews may go in the week time to discuss the Talmud with the rabbi. Jewish people have met to worship and discuss and learn together throughout their history, so it is part of the heritage of being Jewish.

For many Jews, though, the home is a place that it is important. This is because many important festivals are celebrated in the home such as Pesach, Rosh Hashanah and Shabbat. Many Jews show the importance of the home by placing a mezuzah case on the front door and keeping mitzvoth such as kosher food diets. This identifies them as Jewish.

However there are many Jews who don't go to the synagogue but are considered Jewish because one of their parents is Jewish. This is because being Jewish is more than just being a religious Jew. Also for many Jews being truly Jewish is more about the way they act in daily life than going to the synagogue. This would include how you treat other people and how you keep the mitzvoth that are in the Torah, such as 'Do not murder/steal'.

Activity

a Look at both responses against the marking grid on page ix. Which answer would you award higher marks to? Explain why.

b Here is a list of connectives which might be useful in structuring your response. Rewrite Response 2 using some of them to highlight the points you are making.

- Firstly
- Secondly
- In addition to
- Furthermore
- Moreover
- For instance
- To illustrate
- To highlight
- However
- Equally
- Similarly
- In contrast
- On the other hand
- In spite of this
- Therefore
- As a result of this
- Consequently
- Hence
- Ultimately

Exam practice

a What is meant by Shekinhah? (2)

b Describe the main features of a synagogue. (5)

b Describe the main features of a Jewish wedding service. (5)

c Explain why the idea of covenant is important for Jews. (8)

c Explain what Jews believe about the afterlife. (8)

d 'Sabbath is the most important festival for Jews.' Discuss this statement showing that you have considered more than one point of view. (15)

d 'You must follow strict dietary laws if you want to be truly Jewish.' Discuss this statement showing that you have considered more than one point of view. (15)

Notes